AF410667

Searching for Pinky

Searching for Pinky

An Absurdly True Quest
for Motherhood & Family

Alexia Baum

PINKY SAGA, LOS ANGELES CALIFORNA, 2022

Copyright © 2022 by Alexia Baum
All rights reserved
Printed in the United States of America

ISBN 979-8-9855572-0-6 (paperback)
ISBN 979-8-9855572-1-3 (ebook)

Some names have been changed in the interest of privacy.

Published by Pinky Saga
P.O. Box 285
8726 S. Sepulveda Blvd.
Los Angeles, CA 90045

For Stephan,
who never, ever gives up.

And to single mothers everywhere,
too often the unsung and underpaid heroes
of everyday life.

Thank you to:

*My family and the great friends who stood by us
through every part of this crazy adventure;*

*Joyce Wiswell, editor and friend extraordinaire,
without whose encouragement and good humor
this book might never have come to fruition;*

*Eric Larson of Studio E Books,
for going above and beyond;*

*Jason Latif Bozé, who recognized Stephan's unique spirit and smarts
and has continued to support his efforts;*

*and the amazing WISH Academy High School teachers and staff,
who helped Stephan not only recover but excel.*

*Note: The trials and tribulations of this true story began more than 20
years ago, and I am hoping that the treatment of infertility as well as
adoption may have evolved during the ensuing years.*

Contents

I. The Quest

Making Other Plans

IT WAS DURING TURBULENCE at 30,000 feet somewhere over North Dakota, leaning against the 747's cold metal bathroom wall for balance, syringe and needle in hand, pants crumpled down around my ankles, ass bruised purple and yellow like a Santa Fe sunset, when it hit me—this was definitely not what I imagined when I contemplated motherhood.

It had been two years since I had first repeated what had since become my mantra—"I am a happy and healthy pregnant woman." And later, as my pregnancy went awry, my in vitro prospects were dimming, and we began seriously considering adoption, I updated my mantra to, "I am the mother of a happy, healthy child in ___[fill in the year]." I ultimately had to include four or five subsequent years in that blank.

But if there's one thing I'd learned, and sometimes felt like the poster child for, it was the old truism, "Man [*sic*] plans and God laughs." Or as John Lennon said, "Life is what happens while you're busy making other plans."

I was nine months pregnant for five years. That is, I had been expecting, or hoping to be expecting, every second of every day of that time. I watched as friends who weren't even dating when I first started trying met, got married, and had their first and then second kids. I couldn't decide whether I was proud of or aghast at my own increasingly rabid and single-minded pursuit of This One Thing. I constantly dreaded and whenever possible skipped family gatherings, office parties, and birthday celebrations—don't even mention baby showers—as the sheer number of people in my thirty-something age bracket made it a likelihood that at least one pregnant person would be there. I avoided opening pink or blue announcements from all of my married friends. In short, I lived in fear of being side by side with someone else's pregnancy joy when I felt like it was being held endlessly, painfully, inexplicably in front of me like a golden carrot on a stick that I would never be able to reach.

Until you've been denied something that you always naturally assumed was your birthright, you really can't comprehend the blistering, fuming frustration of seeing what feels like every other person in the world enjoying that same right. On a daily basis I cringed when I saw pregnant women walk past, some glowing, others glowering, but all of them in possession of the one thing I knew I wanted more than anything else in the world—a robust, fertile, impregnated belly.

My then-husband David and I had met in our thirties, and I had happily moved from Los Angeles to New York to join him; we knew that we wanted to have children, and I got pregnant less than six months after our wedding. I knew the second I got pregnant; it felt like a gentle starburst inside my body. It sounds corny but I have heard other women say the same thing. I bought a pregnancy test kit and peed on the stick, and when it swelled with color, it affirmed what I already knew.

I called David at his office. "Guess what?" I said calmly.

"You're pregnant," he said.

"How did you know?" I asked, surprised.

"I just knew." I could hear his smile.

I felt like a powerful, magical being, like I was physically gliding through space, beautiful and untouchable. I felt sexy, soft, and overwhelmingly happy.

My doctor confirmed my pregnancy and told me that my due date would be around Thanksgiving. "Sorry, but your Turkey Day food isn't gonna be so great," Dr. Jonathan smiled.

Handsome Dr. Jonathan was about my age and had been recommended by a woman in another doctor's office. I had never worked with a male OB-GYN before—I was much more comfortable with someone who had the same equipment as did I—but I was so thrilled to be pregnant that I was happy to listen to the woman's referral.

"I don't care," I beamed to Dr. Jonathan, "they could feed me gruel and I'd be thrilled just to be there."

They say you're not supposed to tell people you're expecting until you're past the first three months, just in case, but we couldn't keep it to ourselves. We'll just tell our parents and our best friends, we told ourselves. Two hours later we had phoned people from the East Coast to the West and told no fewer than a dozen friends.

But my elation didn't last long. It was not more than a week later that I began having abdominal pains, and a panic rose in the back of my throat. During college years earlier, an emergency surgery had removed an ectopic pregnancy, where a fetus was growing in a fallopian tube, which if ruptured can be fatal. During those college years, they had taken out the swollen tube, along with one ovary that had borne a large cyst, leaving me with one ovary and one fallopian tube remaining. I had been recently tested to ensure that pregnancy was still possible and safe, and the results said it was. But still, I had to safeguard the parts that were left—from the ovary on one side to the tube on the other, pregnancy might not be easy, but it was technically possible!

As I called Dr. Jonathan, the bloating, pain, and bleeding were all scarily familiar. In my heart, I had a sinking feeling of certainty that this pregnancy was too good to be true and was also ectopic.

E for Ectopic

THE FEAR THAT MY PREGNANCY was unhealthy was a constant weight on my psyche, the pain in my gut all too real.

I did another pregnancy test—negative. Then another one—positive. That's what happens with ectopic pregnancies—your body is chemically confused with the pregnancy growing in the wrong place. Then we did a series of blood tests, which we began to do every single morning to make sure my hormone levels weren't swerving dangerously up or down. (After six days of getting stuck with needles every morning, I had learned to ask the nurses to draw my blood as the doctor's touch always left a huge blue welt.)

Dr. Jonathan concluded that the pregnancy was definitely not healthy, that it was likely ectopic, but that given my history and our desire to save my one fallopian tube, as well as the fact that it was impossible to detect an ectopic pregnancy with certainty even with an ultrasound, we had two options. The first was to shoot a chemotherapy drug into me in hopes of dissipating the pregnancy and saving the fallopian tube. If that didn't work, we would do surgery to see if my uterus had anything growing in it. In other words, they would clean out my uterus, and if there was nothing in it, the pregnancy was definitely ectopic, and I would wake up with my one remaining fallopian tube gone. I agreed but called my old doctor in Los Angeles just for a second opinion.

My L.A.-based OB-GYN, a brilliant woman who is tops in her

field, said, "He's crazy, that New York doctor—you don't need drugs, you don't need a test—it's ectopic…just take the tube out and do in vitro."

My mouth hung open. I wanted to ask her how she could be so sure, although in my gut—literally—I knew she was right. And was taking it completely out the only option? And what was this "in vitro"?

Into the silence she said, "Okay?"

"Um, yeah, okay…" I said.

"You can have him call me if you want," she generously offered.

I thanked her and hung up.

With the stakes so high—losing the tube meant losing my ability to naturally conceive a child—despite my gut instinct telling me otherwise, as well as years of bearing witness to my L.A. OB's fast, probably correct diagnoses, I agreed to Dr. Jonathan's suggestion that he inject me with a chemo drug to clear out the fallopian tube. He warned me that it would make me feel lousy. That was putting it mildly.

It was during this time that I decided I just had to attend the wedding of a dear friend in Washington, D.C. even though I had initially declined the invite due to all the medical brouhaha.

"No way, you cannot fly—shouldn't even travel," Dr. Jonathan said somberly after my seventh visit to him in as many days.

"But I can take the train to D.C.—I don't have to fly."

Against my doctor's wishes, I slowly and gently got myself aboard the train to D.C. but took the doctor's beeper number with me just in case.

That weekend, my friend, who had never been especially maternal and who even said that she wasn't particularly interested in having kids (after the ceremony when I hugged her and winked, "Have fun tonight," her mother said, "Make it productive") merely smiled and said quietly, "I'm going off the pill, we'll see what happens…if we have a kid, great. If not, great."

A short time later when she was tired and couldn't figure out why, a friend suggested she might be pregnant. "Huh," my friend laughed. Nine months later her daughter was born.

When I got back from the wedding, I looked very unwell. The chemo drugs had made me bloated and cramped, I was in constant pain from the ectopic pregnancy, my face was chubby and pasty white, hair stringy, and overall I felt like a dying pale balloon with dirty string on my head.

But I made it to the wedding and back home. Charming.

Adventures in IVF

THE CHEMO DRUG they had injected into me had not cured or even affected the pain and swelling in my belly, and so urgent surgery was the next step.

"It was ectopic," Dr. Jonathan told me when I woke up after the procedure, "a large one." And thus my last remaining fallopian tube had been removed, leaving the natural conception of a child impossible.

I was devastated but also relieved not to be walking around feeling like a balloon about to burst. Buoyed by the promise that we were "perfect candidates," I thanks to my one remaining, apparently still hard-working ovary (whom I had dubbed Olivia), we marched naively towards in vitro fertilization, or IVF. We practiced shooting up an orange with a needle as we giggled nervously—it all seemed like a strange and surreal lark, not without excitement, and I was already imagining all the hilarious stories I would tell friends and family in years to come about how little Pinky had been conceived.

I dubbed my child-to-be Pinky—the name derives from *Adam's Rib,* my favorite Katherine Hepburn/Spencer Tracy movie, in which they call each other "Pinky" (one with an "ie" and one with a "y"). I figured that, whether I had a boy or a girl, the name covered both. And certainly IVF was going to be what made Pinky manifest.

Hah.

IVF has become fairly commonplace so I will make a very long, painful, and expensive story short; IVF is not for the faint of heart. It is like strapping yourself into a roller coaster against your better judgement, and the car has jerked away from the boarding platform and begun chugging up an impossibly steep incline. You are certain that gravity will whack the crap out of you and you may plummet to your death, but you are strapped in and there is no turning back—you can literally only go forward with the wish to reach a peaceful ending.

By the time you even begin an IVF cycle, you've usually already been through any number of heartbreaks, both physical and emotional, not to mention financial. And it's probably just as well that no one tells you what to really expect during IVF—otherwise lots of folks might do a rushed U-turn and never look back. But that primal urge to breed—as a woman, it felt like a brand seared into my brain that nothing could ever erase or replace.

The first thing I noticed about IVF was the cost. I was secretly advised by a nurse to buy my drugs from a Canadian or English pharmacy as they would cost far, far less than in the U.S. The cost still ran into the many thousands. And they made it crystal clear that we were to follow the instructions to the exact minute—to veer from the precise timing of administering each drug and/or testing any blood or hormone level could make the whole thing an exercise in futility. I vowed to be the perfect patient and time everything to the second—I didn't want to give *anything* a chance not to succeed!

My heart pounded with excitement—"Just think—we'll look back on this as the beginning of our baby, of our family..." I was absolutely positive that this was the start of something definite, no question of anything not working. No sir, not for me.

How IVF works in a nutshell: First you do a medical consultation (after you have researched and identified what doctor or clinic you are going to work with) and they do lots of baseline blood work and an ultrasound, looking to ensure that your body is capable of success. Then they suppress your hormones and get your ovaries as fattened up as a French goose before Christmas. Then, at one precise moment, they give you the mother of all ovary stimulant shots so that you can produce and then harvest as many eggs as possible. Then they wait for the perfect moment, the peak egg maturation date and time, and retrieve the eggs (you are monitoring yourself and doing almost daily blood work at the doctor's office to keep track), which is done as an outpatient in a hospital.

After they retrieve the eggs, they send them on a date with the man's sperm (the guys get the easy part—simply go into a private room with some porno videos and make their contribution into a little cup, no needles or pain or blood work), presumably in a petri dish of sorts. Once the egg or eggs have fertilized, you undergo the transfer, where the fertilized egg(s) are put back into the woman in another hospital-based out-patient surgery.

And then you wait. For two weeks. This is the crucial time during which you hope and pray that the fertilized eggs are setting up shop in your womb and will transform, nine months later, into a beautiful, healthy, fully formed, delivered baby.

One key step is the pregnancy test that happens at the end of the two weeks after the transfer, and to say it is the pinnacle of all of the many anxiety-producing ordeals is to put it mildly. It is where the rubber hits the road, the shit hits the fan—where you obviously find out whether the physical pain, the emotional trauma, the huge financial cost, have all paid off.

So that first day, before we administered the first IVF shot, I was giddy with excitement and trepidation, certain that this was going to be the beginning of a great adventure and the start of a story I would later tell my child/children (hey, twins would be great!).

I remember standing in the large, lovely bathroom of the Brooklyn apartment we were renting in Greenpoint, right next to Williamsburg. There was a large clawfoot bathtub and a marble pedestal sink, with a floor-to-ceiling window at the far end. The large plastic bag full of needles, syringes, drug vials, and typed instructions was perched on the edge of the sink.

I was laughing and smiling, excited to hit "go" on our baby farming.

There were multiple shots that had to happen a few times a day each; one was Lupron, meant to stimulate egg production, which I started on day twenty-one of my cycle. It was to be injected into the thigh or abdomen with a smallish needle. I found that injecting into the abdomen was actually much less painful than the thigh.

Progesterone was to be injected subcutaneously, or deep into a muscle, which required a much more robust needle. This shot was to go into the buttocks, and to administer it required a steady and determined hand—the worst thing to do was to be timid and only get it halfway in! As first there was no way I would even attempt to administer this shot myself—it required someone standing behind you with a clear aim at your butt. Once the medicine was in, a slow and deepening burning sensation would spread across the whole area, and I could feel the medicine literally seeping into my body.

To ease the injection discomfort, it was suggested that either ice or heat or both could help.

"Okay, let's do it!" I laughed nervously. I decided to do the first shot in the belly myself. I turned over the drug vial, stuck the needle into it, and carefully pulled back to fill the syringe to the exact amount. Then I set down the vial and tapped the syringe gently to eliminate any air bubbles.

"Here goes," I laughed. My pants were around my ankles, my belly exposed, and I took a deep breath. "Okay, here goes," I muttered again, my nerves jangled at best. I pinched a piece of belly and quickly jabbed the needle in. "Ouch!" I resolved to do it a bit more slowly the next time.

"Hmm, not as bad as I thought," I said when I was done with shot number 1 and had dutifully put the used needle and syringe into the large, empty plastic Coke bottle we had secured for this purpose.

There was one shot that could go into my arm, and I let David do that one. He was pretty steady and it wasn't awful.

"Now for the horse-sized needle," I said, watching while David readied the subcutaneous into-the-meat-of-my-butt shot. The needle was seriously large, probably four times bigger than the belly needle.

The drug to be administered was thick and syrupy, and I knew it was going to take some muscle for David to push down the syringe and actually inject the juice into my butt.

I was glad the shot would happen behind me where I couldn't see it—I didn't want to watch that giant thing pierce my skin.

"Ready?" David asked.

"Yup," I muttered as I leaned over the sink, my rear exposed and ready to get jabbed.

"Okay, one, two, three…"

"Owww!" I said as the needle met and pierced my butt, and then another "Owww, owwwww" as David held it there and slowly pushed down the plunger so the syrupy medicine would enter my large butt muscle. Another "Fucking owww!" when he withdrew the needle.

I rubbed my arm and stomach and especially my ass with ice and alcohol and felt very proud of myself and us.

"We did it—we're on the way!" I squealed.

The shots went by, the days turned into weeks—a few times a day, timed to the precise minute, it was one shot in the stomach (still the least painful of the three), one in the arm, and finally the ass-kicker (literally), the horse-sized needle into the ass muscle.

The giant Coke bottle went from empty to partly empty to full and finally to bursting. I had to get another one, and when it got full, yet another. I remember trekking from Brooklyn to the doctor's office on the Upper East Side every morning to both get the daily blood draw (are you ovulating, are the hormone levels right?) and dispose of the detritus of giant needle-filled Coke bottles lest someone see it and think I was a crazed if somewhat well-groomed junkie.

One especially fun perk of ingesting all those IVF drugs were the raging hormones, mood swings to rival Jekyll and Hyde; one day I got lost on the same subway I had been taking every single day for six months, culminating in me screaming at the top of my lungs in frustration, "Fuck! Fuck! Fuck!" as nervous onlookers backed away from me.

And so we marched onward, the daily blood draws overseen by

our sweet but sad young fertility doctor I will call Dr. M., who was supposedly tops in his field. (NYC was full of fertility doctors then, as I imagine it still is today.)

And so our routine continued—me ingesting drugs, me getting poked by the nurses at the clinic daily, me getting poked with more drugs, until finally it was time for the Big Blast, the shot that would skyrocket my eggs into mega-production and ripeness. The day after the Big Blast they would retrieve said eggs, David would make his "contribution," and they would fertilize as many eggs as we decided upon.

A short time after retrieval and then fertilization (we hoped), I would go back in to have the transfer, where the fertilized egg(s) would be put back into me and hopefully grow strong. This was all of course predicated on the assumption that everything had worked perfectly up to that moment—that the hormones and shots had done their job, that we and the nurses had read and measured every-thing correctly, that the Blast had blasted Olivia my one ovary into mega-productivity, and that the stars would then align and my eggs would be happy to rumba with David's sperm. So many details, so much minutiae, with life or not life, success or failure, riding on any single step of the long and complicated process.

The nurse called me the day before to tell me precisely what time to administer the Big Blast shot, which she based on the most recent blood work she had drawn.

"Ten-ten P.M., exactly," she said over the phone. "Got that?"

"Yes, ten-ten," I responded. "Got it."

And so, at 10:10 on the designated night, at the precise designat-ed moment, I poked myself with the one-time-only booster shot that would hopefully inspire Olivia the Ovary to blast out a whole bevy of healthy and potentially fertile little eggies.

My egg retrieval was to be the next day, another out-patient sur-gical procedure at another hospital. (Don't even get me started on what a gigantic and lucrative industry IVF and fertility must be—peo-ple will do crazy things and spend infinite amounts of money when they get on the baby-making quest!)

I remember waiting in the lobby with a few other IVF egg retrieval subjects, one of whom spoke rapidly and easily on her phone about the movie she was working on, the deals she was making, etc. I was amazed at how calm and "normal" she seemed when all I felt like was *wait*—stop the world. Something huge, *monumental* was happening, and it was virtually all I could think or be about.

And then a horrifying thought—maybe this wasn't the movie lady's first go-round? Maybe she'd done this before, maybe a few times before—her presumed husband was staring angrily at his phone the whole time, looking like he'd prefer to be anywhere else on the planet other than right there; they never spoke a word to each other—and maybe she'd become blasé about it.

No, that could never happen to me, no way. This was going to work! I had to believe that or I would have run screaming away from the whole crazy scenario.

And then they called my name and in we went, the nurse comforting and calm. I was sure she had seen everything, all the drama and excitement and heartbreak that this life-and-death procedure could inspire.

The procedure didn't take very long, and afterwards they told us that they had retrieved ten, *ten* little eggs. Wow, Olivia had really done her thing! I couldn't help but feel optimistic.

The next step was waiting between three and five days—closer to five days and the eggs would have turned into blastocysts, a further-along development stage eggs must reach prior to implantation in the uterus—and then I would go back in for the transfer, where a select number of fertilized eggs would be implanted back into me.

Phew! I felt prematurely victorious in having made it successfully to this point.

The days passed and I went numbly through my daily work schedule, David out of town or working his usual thirteen-hour days. I imbued each and every one of the waiting days with huge significance—"This day, November twelfth, will be the day that Pinky started." I was on physical pins and needles, trying to make every step of my daily two-train commute into Manhattan a gentle one, to avoid getting jostled by fellow riders, bustling pedestrians or harried bicycle delivery guys. I darted and wove my way gingerly through the streets, waiting, waiting for the next big day and step in our ongoing IVF process.

The Transfer

FIVE DAYS LATER, we went in for the transfer.

"We have five viable and fertilized eggs," we were told. This was great news! After consulting with Dr. M., we decided that we would implant three, hoping that two would remain viable (twins were a fairly common outcome of IVF). After all, we were still young, my one ovary had worked beautifully, and everyone on our "team" felt optimistic, including me.

And so the three little eggies were implanted back into me—I think it was on Thanksgiving Day, which ironically would have been my due date had my initial natural pregnancy not been ectopic. I opted not to drive upstate for a family Thanksgiving celebration, but to stay at home in bed with my feet raised and let the three little eggs find the right spot to implant and nest.

After a few days, I began conducting my daily business as usual, if a bit delicately.

A week after the transfer, I went in as scheduled for a pregnancy test. They draw your blood (nothing new there) and then you go home and wait. Am I pregnant or am I not? Should I walk up all those subway stairs or not? Can I celebrate, start counting off days to make up nine months or should I soak my sorrows in wine?

"The doctor will call you at seven P.M., sharp," the nurse said. So at 6:59 P.M. I was sitting there, staring at the phone, holding my breath.

When the phone rang, I grabbed it like a hungry lizard snapping up a fly with its tongue. "Hello?" I stammered.

"Congratulations," Dr. M. said, and then went on talking, but I didn't hear anything beyond that. The tears streamed down my face. Finally! Amazing! My dreams and prayers and lit candles and hopes and meditations—they had somehow, miraculously, amazingly, worked!

When we went into the medical office the next day for an ultrasound, there was a heartbeat. What a feeling! I felt like a goddess and a magician and an all-powerful woman all rolled into one.

A week later I was at work in Manhattan and I picked up a very light, small shelf. It was one of those wood-and-wire things that stands about three feet tall and only weighs a few pounds—it was empty at the time, and something I could literally lift up with one finger. But as soon as I did it, I felt different. My stomach started to cramp and I went into a panic. In the bathroom, I was mildly spotting. No, no, no, oh God no, this can't be happening. I screwed up my eyes and tried to roll back time—if I could somehow just make the moment rewind, I could not pick up that goddamn shelf and my world wouldn't be at that moment burning down around me.

I kept the business lunch I had scheduled and watched my lunch date move her mouth on and on and on but couldn't register a thing she was saying.

I got home and called Dr. M. "Don't worry," he said, "something that minor shouldn't make or break anything—a healthy pregnancy can withstand a whole lot more than that—I'm sure it's fine."

When David and I trekked into the doctor's office the next day and they did an ultrasound, the nurse swirled the baton around on my gelled belly but there was no heartbeat. My own heart was pounding so loudly in my ears I doubted they could have heard it anyway. "Are you sure?" I asked, but I already knew. There was no more life in me.

Somehow, I got up off the table and was helped, sobbing, into another room "until I felt better" and wouldn't freak out the waiting room full of still-hopeful candidates, pincushions like me who were pulling themselves through each day just as I had with the promise of a fruitful belly.

I couldn't bear the thought of having lost two children, first the ectopic pregnancy and now this one. David had to make his usual long trek out to Long Island for work so he had to dash away. I was in no hurry to get to the office—there was no way my mind or soul could bear to concentrate that day anyway—so I walked all the way from the Upper East Side of Manhattan to the lower side, near Houston Street, all the while numb, feet throbbing, grateful for the mass of humanity swirling endlessly and anonymously around me on every New York City block, my eyes locked on the gray pavement unfolding constantly beneath me.

Hope

STILL, HOPE SPRINGS ETERNAL, like the Whack-A-Mole game at the arcade; you smash one down and up one pops in another place.

We were reminded that there was no good reason IVF shouldn't work for us, why we shouldn't try again. (I have since come to find out that many people have to do IVF many, many times to have a successful outcome—I wonder what effect all those drugs will have on we women in years and generations to come?) Dr. M. would do it for reduced cost, a kind of two-for-one deal.

After talking to lots of family and friends and doing a boatful of research, we heard of a doctor in San Francisco who was dubbed the Egg Man, a kind of crazy genius of IVF who had gotten nearly miraculous results with loads of clients. Sure, it would cost twice as much as staying in New York, but how could we think of money at a time like this? I could work out of my company's Berkeley office so no worries there.

We decided to go for it—San Francisco, here we come.

IVF Goes to SF

AND SO WE LEAPT INTO IVF 2.0, Round 2. Thus far the score was IVF gods one, me zip.

Before we even embarked for San Francisco to see the Egg Man, there were more needles and more shots. This round even included a weird procedure that necessitated us driving to another state, where they withdrew blood cells from David, spun them out in some strange machine and then, in an effort to negate the possibility that my body would reject his antibodies (I think), they injected them into me.

It's strange but I was by that point so deeply, almost blindly committed to the idea of being pregnant, of bearing a child, that some of the procedural details escaped my usually intently curious mind. I just wanted it to work, it was that simple.

Meanwhile, I daily watched young mothers on the subway yelling at and yanking around their kids and couldn't help but wonder why the world seemed to have so little regard for fairness.

Finally, it was time and I flew to San Francisco—that beautiful city by the bay, where a co-worker kindly let me stay at his cool apartment—where everything went perfectly. Absolutely *per*-fectly. My body responded to every prompt, the eggs were perfect, the transfer was perfect. Even the Zen spa-like vibes and view from the Egg Man's office, which was high up and looked out over the sparkling bay and the Golden Gate Bridge, were perfect.

It felt like every single indicator was pointing to positive, to yes, this was going to work.

When the day came to retrieve my eggs, the nurse exclaimed with happy surprise, "Wow, ten eggs, that's amazing, we never get that many, and all those from one ovary!"

The day of the transfer went perfectly as well, and again we opted to transfer three eggs into me, hoping at least two would take and we might end up with twins. I felt more than calm, I felt tranquil, and was not even angsting like I had the first time. It simply felt right and easier, and I was ready.

David flew back to New York a few days before me for work while I spent time in San Francisco lying on my back with my feet up so the eggs could make a cozy nest inside me. And when I did finally board the plane back to New York, I got to thinking about the whole thing.

For the last year, I had toted around a bagful of syringes and needles everywhere I went. I'd become something of a needle expert. One-and-a-half-inch, twenty-five-gauge, one-half-inch, the small, non-threatening insulin needles. Pink wrapper with heavy plastic. Thin cellophane with black letters. Some from overseas that had a whole different set of markings from the usual "1 cc" or "1.5 cc."

I had felt like Lou Reed must have in the old reckless rock and roll days, and had shot up in bathrooms all over the country, including in between basmati rice and curry chicken at an Indian restaurant on Manhattan's Lower East Side, where I did my needle business in a stall the size of a broom closet. "Miss, are you okay?" the man asked from outside. "Fine, just a second." He looked worried when I emerged ten minutes later, a grimace in place of the smile I was aiming for. Then later in a Stop & Shop just above San Francisco off the highway in the old hometown of the Grateful Dead. I bet that little generic room had seen some serious action in its day.

As I sat there on the 747 heading back home to Brooklyn, San Francisco fading in the lovely rearview mirror, and thought of the whole escapade, I realized that it was time—the exact time—that I had to administer the next round of injections.

There was only one working bathroom for us coach-class folks, and the line stretched stubbornly halfway down the narrow aisle. I could not afford to be late with a single shot so could not wait.

I had to plead with the steward to let me use the out-of-order bathroom. "It's time-sensitive—it's a medical issue," I implored as he handed me the cup of ice I'd requested, "and the line is so long with only half the restrooms working, and…"

"Okay, okay," he said. "Do *not* use the toilet." No problem. I could see the headlines: DRUG-ADDLED WOMAN FLUSHES TOILET AND CAUSES EMERGENCY LANDING IN DES MOINES.

Then he placed a gentle hand on my shoulder and looked meaningfully into my eyes. "Good luck and God bless," he said, as I silently marveled at his lavender mascara and perfect lip liner. "And *do not* flush that toilet!" he admonished.

"Don't worry," I said as I squeezed into the tiny bathroom with my shopping bag full of supplies. Once inside, I tucked my arms to my body to have the space to turn around and lock the door, which would make the overhead light illuminate completely, but the light must've been out of order along with the toilet, since no amount of jamming made it turn on. Then the plane dipped suddenly and that little "bong" sounded, along with the "Please return to your seats immediately" announcement.

The red PLEASE RETURN TO YOUR SEAT sign was the brightest thing in the bathroom, and I leaned towards it as I set down my bag of potions and tools. I dug for the first vial, a small one in a white box, and found it behind the orange-packaged needles, the pink-packaged syringes, and the large plastic pill case filled with individual vials of drugs.

I started with an alcohol swab. The only tidy thing about this whole undertaking was this one neat, little individually wrapped square. I shoved my leg forward to try to keep the overstuffed bag from toppling off the toilet seat and braced my back against the cold steel wall as the plane took another radical dip. "Bong" went the little announcement signal again. "Nice idea—I wish," I muttered when the generic announcer once again told me to return to my seat.

I'd gotten pretty good at this, fortunately, or the bucking 747 would've been too much. I found my small vial and the accompanying insulin needle, swabbed the top of the bottle on its little round rubber circle, stabbed through the top, injected the amount of air equal to the amount of medicine I needed, flipped the bottle, pulled back the plunger, and watched the thick, clear sauce fill the syringe. I pulled out the needle, flicked out the air bubbles, and squeezed a drop out onto the tip of the needle. Glistening there, the drop looked as innocent as morning dew on grass in a *National Geographic* nature shot.

Here goes. I swabbed my belly and reached for one of the ice cubes sloshing around in the plastic cup. As soon as I grabbed it, it squished from my hand. Damn. I grabbed another one, this time with a paper towel. "Gotcha," I said, pressing it towards my belly. (I had discovered months earlier that numb and needles are a very good combination.) But it only dripped there for a few seconds before it too slid from my grasp and disappeared down the leg of my pants. Forget it. Needle sans numb. I steadied back against the cold steel wall to brace myself, took a deep breath, raised my shirt, and aimed for the purple-and-yellow ray of bruises sunsetting out from around my belly button like some sort of psychedelic jellyfish. One, two, three. I stuck the needle quickly into my belly and watched it disappear into my tender skin, squeezed in all the juice, then pulled it out. A small droplet of blood appeared, perfectly round, glistening innocently.

I repeated this scenario with another vial and a much larger needle. This is the shot usually done by someone else. "Intra-muscular" means a very long needle that penetrates the outer layer of fat and goes deep into the muscle, often the buttocks. It's hard to reach and the long needle is hard to voluntarily stick into one's own flesh.

I was amazed again, as I had been yesterday and the day before and the day before that, at how little the needle actually hurt as it pierced my flesh. It was only afterwards, when I'd rubbed the injection spot, thrown away all the plastic wrapping, covered and stashed the needles for later disposal, straightened my face in the mirror, and returned as nonchalantly as possible to my seat, that I felt the familiar warm burn. Ah, yes, that would be the sauce seeping into my system.

As I buckled back into my narrow seat, trying to lean to the non-shot side of my ass, I couldn't help but remember a voodoo priestess I had once visited in New Orleans. After throwing her cat bones onto a hand-drawn chart over and over, she laughed hard and told me that two girls kept showing up. That they would not go away. "I don't know exactly who they are," she said, "but watch." She threw the bones again, and again two of them landed together and away from the others. "See, there they are again." She looked up at me and smiled.

Technology. Voodoo. Prayer. Best wishes. Lighting white candles for hope, red candles for love. Meditation. Not to mention science and the ingesting of every fertility drug ever invented. Funny what you'll try when your heart keeps acting on hope.

"They're coming," the voodoo priestess had said. I hoped she was right.

The Test, the Call

BACK IN BROOKLYN a week or so later and then it was the big day—the pregnancy test. I went into Manhattan to get blood drawn and then the Egg Man doctor in San Francisco would call me that night with the results.

I felt strangely calm. Things in San Francisco simply could not have gone more perfectly. I had done everything I could to make things come out well. The rest was up to the fates. But of course, it still felt huge and my hands were shaking, my palms were sweaty.

The phone rang. I picked it up. "I'm sorry to tell you that…" Once again, the doctor's voice droned on but I didn't hear anything after "Sorry."

When I was able to breathe in and muster my voice back, I asked the doctor why he thought it hadn't worked. "No specific reason," he said.

"Do you think my odds are still good? If I were your daughter or sister, would you recommend my doing it again?"

There was only silence on the phone.

"Doctor?" I asked.

"No."

That was his whole answer. No. That summed everything up, all the pain and angst and expense and schlepping tyrannosaurus-sized needles all over New York City and the country and having to do gymnastics to administer shots on a bucking 747.

No.

I thought of all the drugs I had ingested and wondered if I would wake up one day, maybe tomorrow, maybe next week, maybe in eleven and a half years, and have a hairy breast growing out of my forehead or some dread disease. They really didn't know how and when these drugs might affect women. My family wasn't eager to see me go through it again.

And so, days or weeks later—it could have been a thousand years as I was in a post-IVF, post-pregnancy-hoping coma—I finally stopped *om*ing and *aah*ing and wishing and meditating and lighting candles for a full belly.

I finally let it go.

Then I began imagining a baby, somewhere on the planet, maybe in a womb that was simply her/his temporary home, who was meant to be mine and whom I would no doubt soon meet.

I was going to adopt a baby.

Domestic Adoption

TO BE HONEST, I had not yet been able to fully erase the dream of being pregnant, of birthing a baby myself. And then I went to a meeting of RESOLVE, a national infertility support group with many local chapters with many and various resources, workshops, and support groups.

As I listened to women talk about the joys of adoption, I thought, sure, that's fine for them, but that's not my path—I am going to be pregnant, wear a muumuu, waddle down the hospital hallways… I was shocked to realize I still had all those scenarios on "Play" in my mind.

One RESOLVE meeting featured three adoptive mothers, all of whom had undergone devastating infertility experiences similar to my own. One talked about how she'd gone through five IVF cycles—good grief!—and how her husband had long resisted the idea of adoption, but was now absolutely certain that God had, in the form of their adopted son, delivered to them the one and only child who was meant to be theirs. The other two women said essentially the same thing.

Gradually a lightbulb went on in my head—I had an option. I could choose to let go of the angst I had carried for the past few years, during which I felt like a sad and mournful stranger to my usual optimistic self. As I watched the adoptive mothers sip wine and go laughing into the night, my heart began to open to the idea that my mind had long accepted in theory—that motherhood was more about parenting than being pregnant. The idea that our baby would find us began to take seed—I was ready to embrace the adoption adventure!—followed by a wave of relief as I took the final step off of the infertility roller coaster.

The guest speaker at the next RESOLVE meeting was an obstetrician named Dr. Jane Aronson, who'd long been a schoolteacher who had dreamt of medical school, so had gone at age thirty-five. "I was the oldest person in all my classes," she laughed, her tall, thin frame shaking, her mane of unruly gray hair haloing her face. She became a pediatrician and began specializing in children adopted from other countries, most of which she had visited during her own volunteer work. Later she founded an organization called the Orphan Rangers, where she took med students from her classes at Cornell University to orphanages around the world so they could volunteer their services to these many very needy young patients.

Dr. Aronson seemed to know all the ins and outs of the whole international adoption scene. "If you go to China, to such and such a province, look out for this disease. It won't be a problem, however, if you go to this one." She knew which orphanages in Russia were generally the healthiest, which countries were the quickest or had the worst red tape. I found her objective, clinical yet warm demeanor comforting; she made the whole adventure seem slightly less mysterious somehow. Another layer of the primal desire to birth a child was peeled away—after all, I began to think, it's about being a parent, being loving and kind and there for a child, not only watching your belly swell and imagining what features of yours the child will inherit.

But since international adoption cost roughly $30,000 and took from one to two years, we decided we would pursue domestic adoption, which cost a fraction of that amount and could happen quickly, although there were no guarantees. We knew people who had less money and worse senses of humor than we did, and they had gotten babies via domestic adoption in less than six months. They'd been there for the delivery and everything!

Yep, we were going to adopt a baby domestically, and I was positive that it would happen quickly.

"I am the mother of a healthy and beautiful baby this year. Or next year." My affirmation morphed to fit this new, openhearted me.

Some friends told us about an adoption agency in Vermont which I shall call The Adoption Agency (TAA) and a friend who had enjoyed success with them. In addition, the woman who founded TAA spoke at one of the RESOLVE meetings.

What a relief! Marie, the founder, was an ex-hippie, earth mother type who seemed to speak from the heart, very unguardedly, about the passion she had for adoption and how her life in this nutty world had unwittingly begun.

Having apparently been unable to bear her own children—such a large club, we are—Marie had decades ago tried to adopt. She and her husband, who was Jewish while she was not, had been partners a long while but never married. "You have to be married," said one agency. The next month Marie went back to them. "We're married," she announced in her face-covering toothy grin. "You have to have been married a minimum of three years," they said. She left near tears.

She tried another organization. "You have to both be Jewish," they said. She went elsewhere. "You have to both be Christian," said another. Frustrated, Marie began speaking to adoption authorities and attorneys and learned much of the whys and wherefores of the process. Somehow, she wound her way through the system until someone somewhere got wind of her. I'm not exactly sure how it happened, whether she found a way to "officially" seek an adoptive child or whether a pregnant woman or relative of same heard of her and called her. Anyway, she ended up finding and adopting her daughter.

Marie's unexpected success hit the local papers and spread from there. A short time later, she got a call from someone who knew of a baby boy who needed a family, and she got her son. Her unusual story spread statewide, to neighboring states, and then to New

York. She had suddenly gone from no kids to two babies, and she was still trying to keep her job teaching school. And ever since her success story had gone from local to semi-national, her phone had not stopped ringing.

"How did you do it? I've been trying to adopt for three years, but there's no place that'll help me!" anguished women kept saying.

Marie decided to quit teaching and make a full-time job of trying to help other women become mothers. Thus, The Adoption Agency was born, and over the years they prided themselves on bringing together birth parents with adoptive parents via the open adoption experience, where the pregnant woman picks the adoptive parent(s), they talk, come together (or on the rare occasion, do not), and everything is out in the open, culminating in the adoptive parents going to the hospital when the child is born and bringing him or her home. I imagined lots of happy tears and an unbelievably happy outcome—me cradling my beautiful baby.

I think back on the orientation weekend we spent at TAA's big old comfy farmhouse in Vermont, of the other hopeful couples sitting in a big circle learning about open adoption. "We don't want you to be exhausted, emotional or financially, when your baby arrives," the TAA folks said and I thought, "Oh, how true!"

One man raised his hand. "What percentage of birth mothers change their minds and decide to keep the babies?" I froze at the mere thought. I'm not sure if Marie's answer was vague or if my perspective was colored by the optimism I felt, but I can't recall exactly what Marie said in response. We were made aware that it *did* sometimes happen—you could cultivate a relationship with a pregnant woman for months, talk to her attorney and doctor, pay her bills, fly to meet her and her family, go to the hospital for the birth, and she could still change her mind and keep the baby. She was not asked nor required to sign the adoption papers until after the child was born and any drugs had worn off. Understandably, she had to be in complete consciousness to make such a decision. I could only imagine what a woman would feel once she looked into her newborn infant's tiny face.

I pushed the thought from my mind.

At the end of the weekend, we signed on the dotted line and plunked down our $10,000. We left for home eager, excited about adoption, certain that it would happen quickly for us.

Hooked

WE DROVE HOME and I quickly got to work making our profile, a
four-page, double-sided, glossy brochure about how super-fabulous
we were and how super-fabulous our lives were and how super-great
and lucky any kid would be to be a part of it. It was kind of like a
brochure for a new Ford Mustang or a dishwasher but with our faces
instead of steering wheels or pull-out racks.

Look! Here I am smiling and holding an adorable puppy! Look,
here we are arm in arm in a botanical garden! Look! Here we are
at a happy family Thanksgiving! Man, we looked great. Young and
vibrant and surrounded by a large and loving family. I'd pick us!

I was hooked like a fish on a line, irretrievably committed to the
idea of being chosen, of being good enough (okay, perhaps saintly
enough if you believed our profile) to be someone's mother.

I gathered the photos, wrote the blurb about us. (I felt like a
bachelorette—"Alexia enjoys writing in her spare time, while David
likes to go to the theater.") I made numerous copies—even used
the expensive shiny paper—and sent them off to TAA. I was sure
we'd get a call immediately. Heck, we'd probably have our choice of
pregnant women!

A week went by, then two. I called the agency. "Don't worry, it'll
happen." I stared daily at the quiet 800-number phone we'd had to
install just for the purpose of speaking with potential birth mothers.
It had yet to make a peep.

But still—we were right—it did happen quickly. The first call came from Marie mere weeks after our trip to the Vermont agency.

A young, pregnant women had chosen us from our résumé, and didn't even want to speak with us. She was certain we were it!

"You'd better get ready to come up here right away—you should be ready to leave tomorrow morning to get here by the end of the day." Marie's voice sounded to me like an angel from on high.

The drive to upstate New York would take us about six hours, so that night after work, David and I went to Target to load up on all the baby paraphernalia we would need.

"Jeez, look at this list," I said, confused as we stood amidst a seemingly endless row of diapers, bottles, nursery blankets, and baby carriages.

"Bottles, formula, a warmer for the bottle, a warmer for the baby, receiving blanket…is a receiving blanket different from a regular blanket?" I wondered aloud.

We stood in the wide aisle under the fluorescent lights, wondering which item to choose first. Somehow, we were unable to place anything in our shopping cart. As the minutes ticked by, and then an hour passed, we looked at each other, our faces glum.

"It doesn't feel right, does it?" We both agreed; our gut instinct told us something wasn't right. This was too easy. And the last thing David and I wanted to do was trip over empty baby paraphernalia in our one-bedroom apartment should the whole thing fall through. We left the store empty-handed, figuring we could get whatever we needed as we drove closer to the hospital.

A ringing telephone awoke us early the next morning. We heard the machine pick it up.

"Hi, are you there? It's Marie… I hope you haven't left yet…" I snatched the phone, half knowing what she would say. "We're so sorry—the birth mother's mother talked her out of placing the baby. An aunt is going to raise him. We're so sorry…"

I mumbled something into the phone and hung up, the tears starting to flow. Still, there was nothing for me to say since I had somehow known that this was going to happen. Yet I couldn't help but feel deflated—I had begun thinking of baby names, of how the next holiday season would feel when I too was finally a mom, of how proud my mother would be to again become a grandmother.

With a heavy heart, David flew to California on business. Two days later, Marie called again, urgency in her voice.

"They changed their minds, and now want to place the baby. I guess it was too much for the aunt... You need to come up here right away..."

I called David, who left a work conference and flew back to New York on the first available flight. We laughed, thinking it ironic that he would of course be on the complete opposite coast, the farthest distance from home when the call came.

We spent a sleepless night plotting our drive and whatever Target stores might be open en route along the 350 miles between us and the baby, giddy with anticipation and thrilled that our instincts for caution had been proven wrong. But just before we packed up the car, the phone rang. We looked at each other, dread on our faces.

"It's Marie. We're so sorry, but they decided to place the baby with a neighbor...we're so sorry...it wasn't meant to be...another one will come along soon...go have some fun, you guys are great, we love your resume, blah, blah, blah."

David and I looked at each other. Was this how open adoption was going to go? A carrot on a stick that was forever dangling just before us but always out of our reach? Just looking at the dormant telephone attached to our 800 number made me anxious.

We kept busy at work, and I avoided as many baby birthday parties as I could. David was more stoic, less manic, and seemed to figure—rightly—that all we could do at that point was wait for the right one to come along.

And so it did, or at least it seemed to.

Potential Adoption Scenario Number 2 involved a Birth Mother and a Birth Father—which was unusual; usually the Birth Father was nowhere in the picture—who had a large interest in our religion. As was the norm, Marie called us to give us any pertinent information about the couple and to "prepare" us for the big call/meeting.

"David's Jewish, my parents are Catholics who swore they'd never subject their kids to that kind of dogmatic hypocrisy—what do we tell them?" we worried.

"Be honest," Marie said. And then added with a laugh, "You can, however, be vague."

At Marie's request, we had given her a credit card number so that she could set up a three-way conference call via The Adoption Agency; that way we could all be on the phone—David on our regular phone, I on the 800 number, Marie listening in. We waited by the phone at the prescribed hour and minute, David glancing out the window onto the tree-lined street below, I pacing back and forth across our small apartment. I leapt a foot into the air when the phone rang.

"That's okay, just let it, let it…" David began. He held one phone to his ear as I prepared to pick up our adoption phone. I cleared my throat. "Hellooo," I chirped.

The woman on the other end sounded young. She and the Birth Father were calling from some unknown state in the Midwest.

We said hello, told each other our first names, as we had been coached, and David and I invited them to ask any questions they might have.

"Wellllll," began the Birth Father, "we were wondering what you would teach the baby about religion. We both feel it is the most important part of what they need to learn."

"Both of my parents were raised Catholics," I offered, hoping to score some points. "Though my parents were a bit more open-minded with us three kids."

"My family is Jewish, but we always also had a Christmas tree," David said.

Silence on the other end of the line.

We made awkward small talk for another ten minutes, which felt like hours, and then said our goodbyes. Marie called us back to tell us she thought it had gone fine.

We never heard from them again.

Choo Choo: Welcome Aboard the Domestic Adoption Train

WE STAYED ON THE domestic adoption train—weeks went by, we advertised in a half-dozen places recommended by the agency (Yellow Pages upstate, parenting magazines and the like, each ad usually costing between $400 and $600)—and pretended we were not thinking about the waiting.

And then one day, we got a call from Marie to prepare for a conversation with another pregnant woman.

Potential Adoption Scenario Number 3 involved a Native American woman with whom we bonded quickly and cried on the phone when she told us how "right" we felt, about how we were the one and only choice to parent her baby. "I'm not registered with the tribe…" she said, which we interpreted as meaning that she didn't require anyone else's approval—she had made up her mind and we were it.

Afterwards, Marie assured us that she would get back in touch with us as soon as she got the medical records from the woman.

Days went by. Then weeks. Ultimately, we never heard from her again.

I tried to erase the memory of the woman from the agency who had said smugly, "You know, I just made it my mission, and four months after we started, we had our son." When my sister-in-law gave birth to a girl, I fought off for the millionth time the old feeling that it would never happen for me.

Meanwhile, David's job at an environmental restoration company continued to demand weeks of travel every month, long hours, and a fifty-mile commute each way. Spending lots of hours and days alone and feeling like the quest to become a mother was increasingly out of my control, I became desperate to feather my nest some other way. Like, to *get* a nest to feather, to move out of our lovely but small rented one-bedroom apartment in an industrial and not very friendly area of Brooklyn, to somewhere that could be ours. To a neighborhood that felt more like our planet.

For fun and distraction, I began looking in the paper at houses for sale in Park Slope, then a burgeoning yuppie- and baby-filled area in Brooklyn, reminiscent of the old Ocean Park area of Los Angeles where I had grown up.

Life marched on and Potential Adoption Scenario Number 4 included a Birth Father who wanted his child to be raised playing golf. It was a strange feeling; we had been through a few unsuccessful situations already, so my optimism was slightly tarnished; still, with each new phone call came the hope—and the possibility—that this one could bring our child.

"Do you play?" he asked. David and I paused. "Golf, I mean," the man said. "Teaches 'em what they need to know about the world…"

"No, but we've been wanting to learn," I stammered. The reality is I hate golf. The wasted land, the enormous water guzzling it demands.

The conversation fizzled and the situation disappeared.

We got a phone bill for nearly $500. That conference call with Marie cost 200 and something dollars? We better get a baby quick, I thought, or we'll end up living in a box.

All of a sudden it was Thanksgiving. Again. I couldn't help but remember that the previous year I had been pregnant and my due date would have been Thanksgiving. I tried unsuccessfully to push the thought from my mind.

I turned back to my happy distraction of looking for a house to buy—I had just started a new full-time job in the music business, so knew that we would look good on paper in terms of a mortgage, and I was pining for some aspect of my life to feel under my control—so

I found, battled for, and bought a house in Park Slope, a fixer-upper (more on that later). I figured that it would take a few weeks to fix up the 100-plus-year-old house before we could move in and got cracking to find a construction crew that could make some minor changes.

We started getting holiday cards from friends and family, many of them featuring photos of smiling babies or toddlers in funny poses, some with Santa, some with puppies, many of them posing with their families including mothers who were ten years my junior.

Another childless holiday? Ugh—the thought seemed unbearable.

Still, life had way of delivering little gifts if I could just remain open to seeing them. One night I was battling my way home on the L train during Manhattan rush hour—through Union Square, the busiest and most jam-packed commuter hub of all—and I'd been doing some Buddhist reading so was feeling rather serene. I decided to squeeze to the front of the train so I could actually exit into the station without getting my heels clipped in the huge throng of people. When the door bonged open, I miraculously was the first one out of the subway car and had an unimpeded pathway stretching before me. I started up the stairs towards the next level, where I was to transfer trains. As I turned the corner and looked ahead down the long hallway, I saw a red balloon, one single balloon, floating free, hovering at eye level. As I got closer, still alone in the hallway for the first time in the three years I'd lived in New York, the glittery red balloon hovering right before me at eye level, I saw its big, bright letters in a loopy scrawl: "I Love You." I smiled—this was meant for me, a gift from the universe that something good was in store, someday, somehow, if I could just keep on marching.

Things Fall Apart

IN THE MIDST OF ALL the adoption emotion and chaos, there was one great distraction, and that was the fact that our house was falling down. Literally.

It turned out that the sweet little house I had found had quite a history; the roof had been on fire, the plumbing had leaked into the basement for years, there were gaping holes in the floorboards between the basement and first floor as well as the second and third floors. I had initially planned on knocking down a few walls to make it an open floor plan but we ended up scooping out virtually all the innards of the house.

Days turned to weeks and weeks to months. One day I slogged through the snow down the middle of Brooklyn's Fifth Avenue and opened the front door. The house was utterly gutted, nothing but the four exterior walls.

The dwelling—you couldn't really call it a house—was three stories tall of empty space and the smell of old, burnt wood. No bathroom, no kitchen, no stairs, no floors—*nada*. David was of out of town as usual so I stood there alone.

"Mwahhh, I just bought a very expensive, three-story, two-car garage!" I wailed to myself.

After the shock of staring into my three-story empty box wore off, I resolved that there was nothing I could do but keep paying to have it all rebuilt and put back together.

Potential Adoption Scenario Number 5 involved Amanda and Jonathan, a young unmarried couple in upstate New York who lived with Amanda's parents. After corresponding for weeks and struggling to obtain Amanda's pregnancy and health records, which involved our hiring an attorney (who later made it clear that her $3,500 fee was for a certification and not an adoption agreement, the latter would be a separate and additional fee, and that the worst-case scenario if the situation fell through would be us losing $500 for nothing), after many machinations, harried phone calls, and legal filings for relevant paperwork, rumblings of needing judicial consent (perhaps so the baby cannot be taken back by the mother, it was never entirely clear to me in the whirlwind of chaotic calls), Amanda stopped communicating altogether and eventually disappeared. We were later told that she had relented to pressure from her parents and placed the baby with a local couple.

Potential Adoption Scenario Number 6 involved a young twenty-something unmarried couple named Erin and Mike who both worked in education. We had the prescribed phone calls and they seemed nice if nervous, not surprisingly. We started the official paperwork—requesting health records, consent forms, etc., each transaction bearing a cost to us—and were later told via our agency that we were the people they had chosen to adopt their baby. Hooray! I was of course elated until the lines of communication went increasingly quiet and then faded away altogether. Couldn't our agency TAA do all this reconnaissance work until a given situation was for sure real, and then involve us, I asked? Why drag us through all of these scenarios that keep falling through? "Just hang in there, you guys are wonderful, it will happen for you soon."

Easy for them to say.

And so on we went on rebuilding our Brooklyn house and continuing the adoption adventure.

Potential Adoption Scenario Number 7: We were chosen to adopt the coming child of a woman of mixed race, the Birth Father an African American who was in prison and was against the adoption. Did we have a problem with the race of the child, they wondered? Heck no, we said enthusiastically—my stepfather and stepbrother and step-sister were Black, no prob, we're sure it'll be a beautiful child. Our concern was with the Birth Father—did he have any legal rights, since he was against the adoption? Our attorneys advised us—at $400 an hour—that such a fight could be prolonged for years, with no guarantee that we would ultimately prevail as the parents. And, oh yeah, by the way, we would have to pay the legal costs for the Birth Father as well. We imagined some long, painful legal battle stretching out over many years, and our dwindling resources being bled dry while the child languished in some orphanage. We reluctantly declined, then wondered aloud where the heck the agency was advertising anyway—*Incarcerated Weekly?*

Potential Adoption Scenario Number 8: We received an email from a woman near Guam who invited us to adopt her child, but only after she breast fed him for six months. "You can stay on the island as long as you like," she wrote. Guam?

Potential Adoption Scenario Number 9: We got another excited call from the agency. "We have a new situation, the child, a girl, is already born, and the mother picked you. She's not even considering anyone else."

Whoo-hoo! I was elated! Cautious, but elated. Finally, finally, maybe this was really it—maybe our baby was here after all!

Of course, we asked for details with bated breath.

During numerous conversations, we found out that the Birth Mother was a nurse who happened to weigh 300 pounds and hadn't known she was even pregnant. "I went in for abdominal surgery, and when I woke up, I had a baby!"

"Wow…" we said, feigning enthusiasm, my heart starting to sink, despite the agency urging us to take the baby. How could you be a nurse and not know you're pregnant?

Plus, the baby had been in Intensive Care since birth, and would likely be there for weeks or months—wouldn't that cost hundreds of thousands of dollars? God knows, our insurance company fought us on every single nickel, and they were bound to fight us on this too. I kept thinking about what the agency had said during that first weekend seminar when we had signed up—"We try to get you to the actual adoption with something left in your tank, not exhausted mentally or financially." Hah.

When I asked our agency about the medical costs, they said flippantly, "Oh, they'll cover it, I'm sure!" We sent copies of the baby's medical records to a pediatrician friend so we could get some sense of what she might be facing. It didn't sound good—zero prenatal care, a 300-pound mother, weeks in Intensive Care—and we felt like we had no touchstone, no single authority we could go to for objective and informed advice.

Finally, after hearing from the pediatrician that the risks were unknown but high—"Only time will tell, but I wouldn't be surprised if there were both neurological and physical damage"—we decided we couldn't do it. The risks were too great. It felt all wrong. This was not our baby.

"You need to call the Birth Mother yourself," the woman from our agency said in a deadpan voice. What? Were they kidding? After everything we had already been through?

I did not want to call the Birth Mother—I felt so full of grief that I could hardly breathe in and out, as though my lungs were full of molten lead.

I braced myself and dialed the number. the Birth Mother was distraught. "I thought you were going to be her mommy and daddy," she sniffled. Through tears I told her that we were not prepared to assume all the risks, wished her the best, assured her that the perfect adoptive parents were out there for her, and hung up as quickly as I could.

When it was over, I was snuffling back tears, feeling like we had no one on our side. How could yet another situation be falling apart? Why was the agency trying to force this sick child on us?

When my sister-in-law had her second child, a son, I attended his bris and listened to in-laws gush about how wonderful it all was as I slugged wine and tried to quell the image of the pages flying off a calendar in some 1940s melodrama, and people in the park pointing at me with my eventual baby and saying, "Oh, what a sweet grandmother."

"Just because you want it doesn't mean you're going to get it. No one ever said life was fair." I wanted to tell my therapist to shut up, but I knew what he said was true. "Have you considered child-free living?" he asked. *No,* I wanted to scream. I haven't! I won't! Not me! I'm going to be someone's mother.

But in my heart, I wasn't nearly so certain.

She Says Her Name Is Elizabeth

IT WAS DECEMBER—I was working at my new music publishing job when we got a call that there was another domestic adoption possibility.

"Elizabeth" was a young woman who saw our information online and called us at home. We were told that Elizabeth had an Ivy League degree and that she currently worked in finance.

She wanted to meet, which we did. Elizabeth had shoulder-length curly brown hair and a full, unlined face. She was full-bodied so it was hard to tell if she looked pregnant or not ("I'm just three months along," she said).

After dinner, she suggested we go to a jazz club in Harlem—she has good cultural taste too, we thought—and en route we fully enjoyed her disparaging remarks about our political leaders, a sentiment we wholeheartedly shared. After we dropped her off, we were carefully elated. Smart, funny, politically savvy, into jazz—this child would perhaps share our tastes!

Still, there was an inkling in the back of my brain that this all sounded too good to be true, that things were tied up just a little too neatly in the whole "Elizabeth" scenario…

And the situation quickly grew stranger and stranger. Elizabeth began calling me at ten and eleven at night, crying for hours into the phone as I tried to console her. I was patient and understanding—she could well be the Birth Mother to our child, after all—and

David was always out of town. I began to feel like she was mentally unhinged, or perhaps only had one good screw left holding her together. Plus, Marie was having trouble getting the medical records from Elizabeth's doctor—first they said they never heard of her, then they sent records with no information—and we became increasingly cautious.

Our attorneys joined in and found out that the name she had given us did not belong to the address where she said she lived and to which we had taken her.

One day Elizabeth asked if I would go shopping for maternity clothes with her. "I'm happy to go with you, but you'll be buying them, right?" Marie had warned me to be clear on this before we got to the cash register.

"Yes, of course," she smiled, much to my relief. Maybe I was wrong, I thought—maybe she was not so screwy but just hormonal and scared.

The Upper East Side of Manhattan is known for high fashion as well as high prices, and this boutique was no exception. Elizabeth picked out two or three ensembles—elastic-waisted pants, pretty, large sweaters, each of which had a price tag in excess of $200. I was amazed anyone could or would shop here—you could get the same fashions at Kmart for one-tenth the price—but I deliberately did not blanch.

"So, who's the pregnant one here?" a nice saleswoman asked us.

"I am," smiled Elizabeth. "I'm having her baby."

"Oh my gosh, oh my gosh, that is sooo beautiful! You just made my day! Oh my gosh…" She yelled and motioned for the other clerk to join us. "Come here, come here—look, this lady is having this lady's baby! Isn't that beautiful?"

Elizabeth had ducked into a changing room. I have to admit, I was having a moment. I was imagining how I would tear up with joy every time I relayed this story to Pinky, of how open and marvelous our relationship with our child, and perhaps also with the Birth Mother, might be.

A few minutes later, Elizabeth had chosen $1,000 of maternity wear and we went to the register. "Oh, I left my wallet at the office. Can I come back for these after work?" "Sure sweetie, sure," the woman gushed as my heart pounded. Left it at the office? I thought. How likely is that?

As Elizabeth and I walked down the street towards the subway, she pleaded with me to spend a bit more time with her, and when I said I really had to get back to the office (I'd been gone more than three hours already), she suddenly faux-fainted into my arms. One minute we were walking side by side down the street, the next she was touching my arm, and then she was weaving in front of me and then collapsing into my arms!

I was stunned. I didn't know what else to do so I caught her, which was not easy as she was a large woman.

"Are you okay?" I asked.

Her hand touched her forehead, her face. "Yes," she answered meekly.

Holy shit, I thought, she's really playing this to the hilt, but said, "Okay, good. Why don't you go home and rest. I'll talk to you later." I beat a hasty retreat into the subway with her kitten-like mewing in my ear. "Can't you stay a bit longer, let's talk later, I feel kinda faint..."

I felt terrible for "Elizabeth" or whatever her real name was—clearly she was in emotional distress and was searching for some kind of mother figure, or perhaps for a family to belong to—but the last thing I needed was for some obviously bright, disturbed woman to target me for any reason, unhinged or not.

My heart was in my throat when I got back to the office. I felt like throwing up as I closed my door and immediately called Marie, who had received only another blank medical form from Elizabeth's supposed doctor, and then our attorneys, who would then spend the entire next day (at $400 an hour) discovering that the full name Elizabeth had given us was not only unlisted in New York City, but was not and had never been on the student list at the Ivy League school she had supposedly attended.

I didn't want to admit it, but I knew with certainty that she was a fake. Reluctantly, I called the maternity store that evening.

"Hi, I was in there earlier today with the woman with dark hair, the one who was having my baby?"

"Oh, yes, yes, how are you?" the woman gushed.

"Say, I was just wondering if she ever came back with her wallet to pick up her clothes?" I knew what the answer would be but was still afraid to hear it.

"No, as a matter of fact, she hasn't been back. We're closing in twenty minutes, but you can always come back tomorrow..."

I didn't hear the rest of what she said, but hung up the phone, knowing it was over.

The next day I called our whole team—Marie, our attorneys, the social worker—and told them it had been a hoax. That night Elizabeth called over and over and left long, teary messages on the machine; with David still out of town, I started wondering if Elizabeth was going to show up on the doorstep with a knife. She was smart and desperate and unhinged, and I was afraid of her; for weeks I looked nervously over my shoulder on every subway platform and street corner, haunted by the constant image of Elizabeth looming towards me with a knife aimed at my heart.

Pining for Motherhood

AND SO IT WENT ON… The next woman to pick us (by now it was starting to seem unreal, just more like an exercise in futility and absurdity), was Maryann.

Maryann lived in Utah, was thirty-three years old, and was pregnant with her fourth child. One child's dad was a junkie in prison. The unborn child's father was merely a ne'er-do-well and was under house arrest. In one phone conversation Maryann asked if we had picked out names (she was pregnant with a boy). I didn't say anything but thought…Stefan. Chandler.

Things got weird with Maryann. Her sister called our adoption agency to tell them what a manipulator Maryann was. It was a risky situation—would Maryann even end up placing the baby for adoption? Would the Birth Father freak out and demand money or the child or something else?

Meanwhile, I marched numbly on, feeling great one day, like everything was possible, spring sunshine lighting the world with a golden hue; by the next day I might feel utterly hopeless, like I was barely clinging to my sanity. It felt like I was choking on a furball of pain, anger, angst, and bewilderment. I understood why people turned to religion, something I was never able to fully do, despite being enamored of the inspiring buildings, the pomp and circumstance, and the theatrics of the church. Out of desperation and a desire not to have to feel responsible for things—"it's out of my hands," my religious friends would say—I wished I could believe like they did.

It was almost April and it was snowing. Hard. I was forced to stay inside the small rental apartment we still occupied while the house in Brooklyn was on month six of being torn apart and put back together.

At work, I was asked to make a priority of getting a misogynistic rap song into a new TV show about pimping and how hard it was on the men in charge. "Hah, you're kidding, right? Is there really such a show?" They were not kidding.

On the home front, I felt like a fish out of water with my social-climbing in-laws—what china pattern did so-and-so pick for her wedding? Who hired the best caterer for the upcoming holiday meal? How many carats was so-and-so's engagement ring? David was out of town most of the time as usual and so I continued to pretend that I felt like one of the family, but in truth I felt like a square peg in a round hole.

We were asked to send Maryann some cash for "acceptable" expenses related to her pregnancy. We did. She disappeared. I guess it was no surprise.

Next call was from Lindsey in Enid, Oklahoma. She was nineteen years old, said she was not sure who the baby's dad was, "a white guy or a Mexican guy, but neither one is my real boyfriend." I told the agency that it didn't feel right; they had our attorneys call her (they billed by the quarter-hour), and afterwards she disappeared.

Summer arrived. Prospect Park was gorgeous, dogwoods blooming everywhere. I adored the neighborhood, the huge, elegant brownstone apartments lining both sides of the tree-lined avenues; quaint, brown-suited old men feeding pigeons from park benches; bodegas where the owners might speak a language you have never even heard of before. I loved every single thing about it.

We crept into August and the drone of summer. A friend—the one whose wedding I had attended when I had the ectopic pregnancy—wrote a book that got optioned for a movie and was pregnant with her second child and living in an exotic locale. I was thrilled for her, proud of her, but in comparison I felt like an old vinyl record stuck on repeat, going round and round in the same old groove but never advancing into a new one.

And then came fall and 9–11. I was in Toronto for work at the Film Festival when the planes hit. With some fellow New Yorkers sequestered in our hotel rooms, we watched the reports in increasing disbelief. Days later I managed to get a train home; it was jam-packed, they ran out of food and water, we had to stop often, including at Niagara Falls, to let bomb-sniffing dogs board the train and sniff through every car. Still, we all bonded with our fellow passengers, sharing our crackers and warm beer and generally hanging on to the nearness and warmth of our fellow humans.

With all the stops and security checks, it took days to get back to New York City, and I finally arrived to a deserted train station at 4 A.M., the city silent and surreal. I caught a cab home to Brooklyn, all the streets quiet and lifeless, the cab driver shell-shocked. We were all shell-shocked.

The reality of the event sank in slowly, from "Missing" posters plastering every available wall space, to vigils and memorials. Grief hung over the city. One neighbor lost her mother, who had worked in one of the towers. Another lost his son (unimaginable). Another friend survived but was so traumatized that he didn't leave his apartment for six months. Our local Brooklyn firehouse lost all of their firefighters. *All* of them.

But one day still turned to another and our house got built and eventually the holidays arrived. My mom and sister came to visit and we had a lovely time in the new house.

And then it was a new year. Thank goodness.

We had left our house as a two-unit building when we bought it—the top 2 floors our house, the bottom floor a basement apartment—and one of David's co-workers, a Brit named Jason, moved into the bottom rental unit, a cute little studio/garden apartment.

Shortly thereafter, Jason invited his girlfriend Sonya to come over from the U.K. and move in. Shortly thereafter, Sonya got pregnant. Then they adopted a large, mean, loud dog, all without asking us. Neighbors would cross the street to avoid walking by our yard.

"They really can't all fit in one small, if charming, studio apartment," I said, insisting David tell them they needed to move. He wouldn't, he couldn't do it. I made it clear that they had outgrown the space and offered to tell them myself, but David implored me not to do it.

Sonya, being British like Jason—who had been seeing a string of different women up until the actual day Sonya had arrived—had a heavy English accent. She would sit on the lower stoop step, slowly peel oranges, and proclaim everything "gorgeous," drawing it out so it sounded like "gawww-jusss." "Oh, look at that kitty—isn't that gorgeous?" "I went for a walk—it was gorgeous."

I gritted my irritated teeth and stepped around her as I bustled off to work.

Riding the subway into Manhattan, I thought of the three or four long years—it felt like a lifetime—that I had been trying to become a parent, but thus far had experienced nothing but disappointment and heartache. And mountains of bills. I couldn't help but recall the RESOLVE meeting where Dr. Jane Aronson had spoken, telling us about how many hundreds of thousands of children all over the world were dying (often literally) to find forever families and homes.

I was ready. I was done with the craziness, the fruitless carrot on a stick of domestic adoption—I was going to adopt internationally.

I started doing research and talking to agencies—we considered Mexico but they said it could take years. Same with China. "Russia is fairly fast right now," an international agency rep told me. "Great! My mother's family is Russian, cool coincidence!" I said. What a relief to feel enthusiastic and hopeful again, to have a destination I could steer towards.

As I told TAA, our domestic agency, I didn't want to adopt a crazy pregnant woman, I wanted to adopt a child. It was going to cost another small fortune, and I would have to recompile every single document of our lives once again, but at least I would never have to talk to another confused maybe-or-maybe-not Birth Mother!

Strolling through Prospect Park, I came upon a Russian winter festival. I took this as a sure sign of good things to come.

I found an agency that did loads of work in Russia—we will call them RAA, or Russian Adoption Agency—signed the papers, and started filling dozens of files with copies of our documents, which included original birth certificates, medical records, college transcripts, lists of all the places we'd lived for fifteen years, requests for high-level security checks, etc.

One week later, sitting amidst a pile of papers and documents and files, I got a call from TAA in Vermont—a young, pregnant women in New York had chosen us, and the agency swore that this one was for real.

The Last Straw

I HELD MY BREATH when the woman from TAA started to speak before I even said hello into the phone.

"We know you're now planning on adopting from Russia, but we got a call from a pregnant woman upstate who has chosen you, and she swears that she is not even considering or speaking with anyone else. She's six months pregnant, she'll call you later."

I came to find out that her name was Karlie, she was a teenage college coed who got pregnant with Sam, her boyfriend. Her mother and father were in the picture and supposedly supported the adoption idea, as did Birth Father-to-be Sam.

That night, we had a great conversation with Karlie, who sounded young and sweet but pretty together. She said she liked our résumé, especially David's having mentioned the Yankees (turns out her mother, wearing the expensive satin version of a Yankees jacket, was an even more fanatical fan than David), and our whale-watching picture. "My aunt used to take me whale-watching," Karlie laughed. It was happening again—my heart was starting to skip beats, to imagine coming through our front door with a small bundle of my own, to fantasize about birthday parties and all the events we would share over the coming years.

Before we hung up, Karlie said, "I want you to be the parents of my son." She had found out that it was a boy, and I could hear that she was pleased with herself at having said these words. I was thankful for the apparently good counseling she was getting. I choked back tears and told her what a beautiful thing that was to hear those words, how appreciative we were, what an honor it was, etc. We hung up thrilled—it sounded so great, and we actually liked her. Perhaps we would really end up with a baby after all!

In our follow-up conversation with our agency, they said that Karlie and her mother would like to meet us. We hastily arranged to fly upstate to Rochester and meet them for dinner that weekend. I watched the New York ground fly by below us, dappled by the plane's moving shadow as the city faded into slowly spreading green hills, then brownish weather-proof tundra, then finally green again as the plane descended into Rochester.

As we descended towards the tarmac, I couldn't help but imagine coming home with my own baby. I almost couldn't imagine it actually happening, it had been nothing but a fantasy for so many years. And then I flashed on our downstairs tenants, in our now very crowded studio apartment rental unit, where my worst nightmare was suddenly coming true—our tenant's girlfriend was heavily pregnant. "We didn't want to tell you until we were sure and some more time had gone by—but guess what, we're pregnant!" When they told us they had leaned in to hug me but I was numb, my arms hanging by my sides. So that's why she's been hiding from me every time we threatened to bump into each other, I thought. I had stepped back and looked down—yes, she looked pregnant and not a little. "When are you due?" I had asked, feigning enthusiasm.

"You're not going to believe this," she grinned, "but in about seven weeks!"

"Greattttt," I had said and made an excuse to leave.

Later I was aghast. "She's pregnant? In *our* house? No. No way, not here—this is the one single place on the planet where I am supposed to *not* have to deal with pregnant women!"

David had assured me half-heartedly that he would talk to them about finding a different place—one that would work for three people and a huge, mean dog—but I knew that he likely either never would or would be apologetic and make it easy for them to ignore the request.

I had started peeking out the front window before coming or going from our house to make sure I never crossed paths with our pregnant tenant. I could hear her perched on the lower stoop, peeling her oranges and declaring everything "gawww-jusss."

I shook myself back to the present as the plane bumpily touched down. Maybe now it will finally be my turn, I thought.

In Rochester, we met Karlie and her mother in the parking lot of the Cheesecake Factory, Karlie's "absolute favorite" restaurant. She had amazed us with tales of how much she could eat, two plates of pasta and three desserts at a time. They were both sweet, Karlie with a pretty, pudgy, round baby face and long, brown, semi-wavy hair that reminded me of a princess from a fairy tale. Her mother was very no-nonsense, funny, short, and sturdy, curt but in a rather charming way.

We ended up at the hotel restaurant when the wait was too long at the Cheesecake Factory—apparently it was the best culinary game in Rochester—and shared an enjoyable meal. Karlie's mother and David talked about the Yankees, we chatted with Karlie, she seemed relaxed and the whole thing felt easy.

We left with hugs all around and went back to our hotel cautiously elated. I was beginning to think of baby names and flew home the next day trying to keep a lid on my happiness, knowing all too well that we still had a long way to go.

The next day, a Monday, our agency called and said that Karlie would call us by Wednesday or Thursday to set up a time for us to talk to and/or meet Sam, the Birth Father, who lived a mere hour upstate rather than the eight hours away that Karlie did. It just seemed to keep getting better, more solid, and against my better judgement, I allowed myself a moment of true elation, a sense of inevitability much like what a healthily pregnant woman must feel, of wanting to announce our due date (June something), of planning for the imminent happy arrival of our first baby.

Waiting on Karlie

KARLIE DID NOT CALL by Wednesday. Or Thursday. Or Friday. I called our agency, who said they hadn't heard anything either but felt there was no reason to worry. I was sleepless despite their assurances. How could they possibly say that there was no reason to worry? Had they forgotten all the lousy situations we'd already been through? I was constantly on the verge of losing it, working desperately to maneuver on the tightrope between hope and despair, between pursuing Karlie and her/our baby boy and entirely ditching the continent for Russia, where as far as I knew no nutty pregnant women or incarcerated fathers could weigh in on whether I became a mother or not.

I checked to make sure the phone still worked—it did. Two days later, when we still hadn't heard anything, I spent hours trying to reach a phone repair person, only to have them assure me that the phone was *still* working just fine.

When Karlie had not called by Saturday, I was bereft. Could this scenario too be wavering towards a horrific end? How could Karlie and her mother have seemed so happy, so sure, and now have suddenly just disappeared?! Our agency had not received any papers, medical or otherwise, and had left numerous messages for Karlie with no response. On Sunday night we left a message for Karlie, trying to sound very lighthearted and jovial. "Hi Karlie, it's Alexia and David, just wanted to say hello and see how you're doing…we're looking forward to catching up again soon…" My heart was pounding a million miles an hour, and I hoped that my rehearsed words sounded like more than a desperate squeak.

David left town on yet another business trip, and I spent from sunrise Saturday morning to midnight on Sunday night fluffing the house. I drove to Ikea and lugged home a stupidly heavy commode and bookcase that took about ten hours to assemble, I scrubbed the bathroom to a shine, cleared out the closets, recycled every scrap of paper that had accumulated over the months, did every piece of laundry (including some pieces that were already clean), and sewed curtains for the kitchen. By Sunday night I was exhausted but felt as though I had at least made some sense of our home space and had put our physical surroundings into order. Since the thing I then wanted most in the world—motherhood—seemed out of my control, at least I could control some small piece of my physical world.

The next week I got to work early every morning and stayed late every night, trying to surf my mood waves without wiping out. The highs were welcome—life is good, everything will work out, it wouldn't be so bad to be able to go to Europe one last time sans crying kid—but the lows seemed bottomless, and I felt like motherhood was being held torturously just out of my grasp. *How come every eighteen-year-old loser on the subway can pop out babies like biscuits, and I have been trying for years to become a parent? It's not fair!*

I plowed my way through my business days and nights, including midnight phone calls to inquire whether our superstar pop princess could include the word "the" in a multimillion-dollar commercial for an internationally renowned soft drink.

"Hi, how much would it cost to license that big song for a diarrhea commercial?" Some days I couldn't decide whether to cry or laugh out loud, and often did both.

I would juggle calls with clients, negotiating $100,000 deals for ten-second snippets of a song in a commercial for racy women's lingerie, along with calls from our adoption agency. I'd say "Hold on, hold on, I'll be right back," go back to try to take seriously the screaming agent, attorney, or songwriter on the other line, then back to what I considered reality—my quest for motherhood.

By noon most days, my head was swimming, and I fought the urge to leap into a martini glass. Still, I didn't want to be a martyr; lots of people had it way worse than me. I had good health, a lovely home, an enviable job. And what about the wars raging all over the globe, the mothers and wives and sons who had lost family, each other, their own lives? I told myself that I had to snap out of it.

I told myself that things would work out fine. If this baby, whatever crazy number it was, was meant to find us, he would. I promised myself that, by hook or by crook, despite David's resistance, I would not watch our tenants go through Babyville if this next baby of ours fell through.

On some dark days, after having temporarily given up hope, I would talk myself back into the game and resolve to let things take their natural course. Often I would swing from elation to depression many times a day, and sometimes within a twenty-second period.

And then seemingly out of the blue, our agency finally called to set up a conference call between us, them, Karlie and Birth Father Sam. It was to be at 3:45 P.M. sharp. Again, I tried to quell the images of walking through our front door with a baby in my arms, and after a sleepless night, got up around 5:30 that morning, thinking how comforting it was going to be when I finally heard that young man's voice. Maybe then this whole thing would seem real. I reminded myself for the fifteenth time that we had not yet even seen Karlie's medical records, not to mention her general family history papers (physical and mental health, genetics, etc.). Our entire relationship to that point had been based on one very mediocre shared meal, a few promises, and my desperate though flickering sense of hope.

At 3:30, I closed my office door. "Angie, no matter what, no matter when, do not miss that call." My assistant nodded seriously. As if I was even going to consider leaving my chair until the call came.

Finally, the call came. It was Marie from our agency. Then she connected David from his office via the AT&T operator she had engaged specifically for this occasion. Finally, she tried Karlie's phone (it was from Karlie that we would get Sam's number, as she had not yet given it to anyone since she protected and coddled him as though he was a child, which he actually was). Karlie's phone rang until the machine picked up.

My heart plummeted. Marie said cheerfully, "Well, it's a beautiful day, she's a college kid, maybe she's enjoying the outdoors." "Mmm," I mumbled, sure the whole thing had crumbled, that Karlie had changed her mind, that the boyfriend was avoiding the situation, and that the whole possibility was about to dissolve, just like so many had before.

David and I went to our counselor—life was challenging enough in those post 9–11 days, with David constantly traveling, our house repairs, my crazy job, then throw in our baby quest—and talked about all the ups and downs of the recent days and hours, from joy to the pits and back and forth countless times. As I recounted some of the many details, I was amazed to realize just how much had transpired, changed, un-transpired, and re-emerged in different form in a mere few hours. It boggled the mind. I may be a mom soon, in a few weeks, really, and I had no diapers, no crib, no blankies, a very full-time job, a workaholic husband—how exactly was this going to happen? And I had no swelling belly to force the readiness, the slowing down, the tending of the nest, which made the parenthood possibility feel like some absurd poker game—will they or won't they win the big prize? I tried to ignore the possibility, but was aware that this baby too might disappear.

I left the counselor's office feeling strong but vulnerable, sure that I was being asked, by David, by our attorneys, by Marie at our adoption agency, even by the circumstances themselves, to stay detached from something that was surely the single area in life about which I felt distinctly the opposite of detached. Motherhood. I would feel that way even if this was Scenario Number 1, and our hearts and minds and wallets were intact, which they were most definitely not.

I heard on the news that a twenty-something starlet and her newly blond husband had adopted a baby from Cambodia. Goddamn rich and famous, I thought as I disappeared into the subway, glad for the anonymity of the swirling crowd.

Finally, after setting up another date and time for the Phone Call, we spoke with Karlie and Birth Father Sam, who seemed about like what you'd expect from a tall, sullen, sweet but still childlike teenage father-to-be. Though they were predictably vague—typical teenagers—everything seemed to be on track. No one seemed to be changing their mind about our adopting the baby, and they wanted us at the hospital after the birth. When the time came, we were to pick up Sam en route since he lived between us and Karlie.

When we hung up, I was thrilled but still cautious. It seemed too good to be true, but there it was—the right words had been spoken, we were going through all the motions, yet I felt somehow numb.

All that was left to do was wait for the baby's arrival.

I Hate Rochester
(or, I'll Never Look at
Lilacs the Same Way Again)

"SHE'S GONE INTO LABOR." The call came late one spring evening when David was, as usual, away on business. As I launched into production mode—with a background in the film and music industries, I was good at doing a hundred tasks at once, all under pressure—I guess my caution was finally thrown aside. This was it! Our baby was coming, everyone was on board, preliminary papers had been signed (of course, the Birth Mother couldn't sign adoption papers with finality until after the birth of the child), and I allowed myself to feel excited. I was finally going to be a mom!

I took a cab to the airport to pick up a rental car that we could all fit in, along with our luggage and baby paraphernalia, which we had finally relented and bought. After the cabbie got lost for forty minutes, I found the rental office, got into the car, drove home, loaded it up with our clothes, the baby seat, bottles, a blankie, and assorted other goodies, and drove back to the airport to pick up David, who had flown home overnight so that we could then drive the six hours upstate to Rochester and directly to the hospital.

We picked up Birth Father Sam at a modest apartment complex in the wooded hills an hour or two north of New York City. He was tall and gangly, a lovely young man, one parent African American and one Japanese. His six-foot, three-inch frame barely folded into the backseat, we made some small talk en route until we got the call.

"The baby was just born—it's a boy."

David and I were in tears, we were beyond thrilled; Sam's expression changed. "Wow, I feel—different." I wondered privately at his expression—it had pride in it, and despite his youth, a giant caution flag went off in my head. I recalled the last conversation I'd had the night before with our agency; when I had asked them if one of them would be there in case we needed assistance, emotional or otherwise, they said, "No, you guys are great, you can handle it. Besides, the social worker at the hospital has been working with Karlie and says all is well." It had seemed so simple, too simple, but they were the pros, after all, and in my excitement I simply forged ahead. Besides, what else were we to do?

Rochester, New York, is closer to the Canadian border than it is to New York City, and it is a city that looks partly passed over. The suburban outskirts are flat and bleak, a post-industrial area, while the downtown area has some mild charm, including some lovely gardens, the city being known for its roses.

We arrived at the hospital and asked whether Karlie and Sam needed some time alone, but they said no and ushered us right in to meet the baby. Karlie and her mother happily and immediately passed him, a tiny little brown bundle, into my arms. I teared up, they snapped photos of David and me with him, Karlie's mom gave us the newborn hand- and footprints on large pieces of paper. It all felt surreal. Eventually we left for our hotel, the plan being that we would go home with the baby a day or two later.

We called our families. "He's here! He's beautiful, he'll be tall, we're going to name him Sean."

Plans were made for flights and visits and toasts; happiness seemed to rain down on us. At their request, we ordered and delivered barbecue for Karlie and Sam, spent some evening time at the hospital, kissed the baby, and went back to the hotel. We bought champagne. "This will be our last night as non-parents," I remember saying. We looked at each other, stunned and excited. It still felt surreal, almost as though I was watching it happen and not actually living it.

The next day we visited some more and got diapering lessons

from the nurse, all of the staff congratulating us on the adoption and making us feel welcome. Karlie and her mother seemed happy, no danger signs except a distant unease in our guts. Karlie's mom casually mentioned that she had borne and lost a baby boy twenty years earlier, and another danger flag waved before my eyes—why had no one mentioned this? Was our agency, the social worker, even aware of it? To me it seemed huge. I knew only too well how searing and permanent a loss like that can be to a mother or prospective mother. As a woman, I knew that this meant that she had unfinished mothering business, and here was another baby boy…still, there were smiles and assurances all around.

That evening as we were leaving the hospital we saw "Sean" screaming in the nursery, writhing and red-faced, with no nurse in sight. We stopped hesitantly, then walked to the nurses' station where someone appeared.

"Excuse me, that is the son we're adopting, can we go in since he's screaming and all alone?" The on-duty nurse smiled warmly and said sure, go on in.

We walked in and I picked up Sean and sat down in a rocking chair. He stopped crying. We sat that way for a minute or two, the darkened evening hallways quiet all around us, until the nurse shot an alarmed look and said, "You've gotta go, gotta go right now." She grabbed the baby from my arms and placed him back into his tiny bed.

"Wha?" we asked as they ushered us out. "What happened—is something wrong?"

Another nurse appeared. "Karlie is upset, she's crying, distraught…"

"What? Why?" My heart stopped, then sank. I knew this was too good to be true.

"Karlie's mother saw you holding the baby and told Karlie, who got upset. You should leave now…"

"But, but…" I began, "the nurse said we could go in! He was screaming!"

We were ushered out, confused, upset, angry. "We have to do

something, quick," I said as we drove to the hotel. We spoke in quick succession to our agency and the social worker. Everyone agreed that the nurse should not have let us into the nursery. "But we didn't do anything wrong!" I literally cried. "Someone should have told us what was okay and what wasn't!"

To his credit, David seemed more angry than worried. "Fucking social worker," he seethed. The man had earlier said with a smile, in front of Karlie and family, "Gosh, the baby doesn't look like a 'Sean.'" We had been discussing doing some sort of small ceremony prior to leaving with the baby the next day. I had wanted to slap him for being so glib.

"Is this still going to happen? Maybe we should just leave," David said. The thought had crossed my mind too but I was horrified to hear it said out loud.

"No, no, I think things will be okay," the social worker said. We hung up the phone afraid that our unintentional faux pas had cost us the baby. Still, in what little was left of my logical brain, I thought of the tiny shelf I had lifted ending my IVF pregnancy and the doctor's remarks that a healthy pregnancy should withstand much harsher treatment than that. Shouldn't a healthy open adoption be able to withstand the adoptive mother holding the baby, especially since the Birth Mother had practically shoved him into my arms days before?

We wondered aloud why we had been left high and dry, with no backup from our agency or the useless social worker, no one to steer us through this long and confusing emotional minefield.

"The agency always said we needed a plan, that we needed people on our team because it could be so rife with emotional danger... where the hell are they?" I fumed. "And how could they not have known that Karlie's mother bore and lost a baby boy? Hello, talk about danger signs!"

I didn't sleep at all. All night my chest burned with every breath and I tasted bile in my throat.

If It Quacks Like a Duck...

THE NEXT MORNING, we went back to the hospital with sleepless and heavy hearts. We had been instructed that we needed to apologize for unintentionally crossing some invisible line, after which we would supposedly leave for home with the baby. The social worker insisted that everything was fine, but it felt urgently not fine.

We had spent an hour installing the infant seat in the backseat of the car, and finally pulled up in front of the hospital doors, as instructed, baby seat secured.

I was nauseous, nervous, and felt like I had been accused of murder or something else unforgivable.

But still I had gone through all the motions of bringing a newborn baby home—we had filled baby bottles in the diaper bag, a half-dozen onesies, snuggle blankies, tiny socks, the works. We were ready to go in, sign the papers quickly, load our son into the car, and get the heck out of there.

The social worker met us in the hallway. "Karlie's very upset, very upset..." I couldn't stop crying as David and I, Karlie's mother, and the idiot social worker were ushered into a broom closet for privacy.

Through sobs, I managed to squeak out, "I'm so sorry, we didn't mean to upset you, the last thing we would want to do is hurt Karlie's feelings..." No one mentioned whether this was actually still going to happen or not, but it sure didn't feel like it. When Karlie's mom went to join Karlie and the baby in Karlie's room, we begged the social worker for clarity. "This is not going to happen…" David muttered.

"It feels horrible, everything is wrong," I cried.

"No, no, everything is fine, we're still on track," the social worker said. Maybe on his planet, I thought, as his words sure didn't seem to match the situation *we* were in. We followed him to Karlie's room anyway. Repeat performance of tearful apologies all around. Karlie sat in bed cradling the baby, tears streaming down her face. Sam sat sullen and silent in the corner.

An absolute, living nightmare.

The social worker stepped over and rubbed Karlie's shoulder. "Do you want David and Alexia to leave for a minute?" Karlie nodded, tears still streaming down her face. I would have been happy if the ground had opened up and swallowed me at that very moment.

The social worker ushered us out. "Karlie needs some time to say goodbye privately. Why don't you wait in the garden next door, and we'll call you in an hour or so…"

I couldn't think of anything to say so said nothing.

My mind reeled; Karlie had been crying so much that she couldn't even speak, I had been sobbing, Karlie's mom was crying—it had been a real fun fest.

We stepped out into the hallway, the social worker behind us. He gently closed the door. I felt so mishandled and badly represented and misunderstood! They knew nothing about us; we were not insensitive cretins! We had trodden through hell to get to this point and didn't deserve to be in this horrifying situation!

The emotion and anger swirled inside me. I thought but of course did not say, *We wouldn't want to freaking bruise Karlie's tender little feelings, now would we?*

I muttered, "She's so emotional and obviously looks super-upset. This doesn't look or feel right…" I couldn't help but think of something a therapist friend of mine used to say about obvious situations we were reluctant to see clearly: *"If it walks like a duck and quacks like a duck, it's a goddamn duck!"*

And this situation—Karlie, the inept social worker, the weird mother who had a dark and untold history, our agency leaving us dangling out there alone in a very scary and dangerous place—this was definitely a goddamn duck.

The social worker chimed in, "Oh, no, this kind of emotion is normal…she's just saying goodbye. This is nothing to worry about." David and I looked at each other—*what planet is he on? What has he been smoking?* Karlie was clearly distraught and even a blind moron could see that things looked dicey at best.

"Why don't you go get something to eat and we'll call you to pick up the baby in an hour."

We stumbled, numb and confused, out of the hospital, past our parked car, and headed a few blocks up a hill to a beautiful park with rolling green hills on which dozens of lilac and cherry blossom trees were in magnificent full bloom. It was the Weekend of Blossoms or something like that and tourists from all over the country and the world had come to enjoy the flowering splendor.

Rochester, New York is known as the Garden City, and one of its highlights is Highland Botanical Park, 150 acres of lilac and cherry trees as well as a myriad of other gorgeous plants, all set amidst beautiful winding pathways as designed by Frederick Law Olmsted, of Central Park and Prospect Park fame.

We walked like zombies in between the magnificent trees, the lavender and lilac smell wafting through the air, gentle pink petals blowing through the soft breeze and swirling slowly around us, as though they were the confetti remnants of a sweet parade. The beauty of the place seemed almost mean given how trampled I was feeling.

We plopped down onto the grass under a perfect cherry tree and picked at green blades of grass and held our cell phones over our heads and twisted them around every five minutes to make sure we were getting reception. God forbid we should miss the Call.

After twenty or so minutes, sitting still became impossible. We walked slowly down the hill towards a greenhouse. Might as well check out the flowers. Someone took our picture standing under a particularly spectacular cherry tree and we managed sickly smiles.

We were surrounded by happy couples, snapping away under the ridiculously gorgeous trees.

We both held up our cellphones. Nope, nothing yet.

We stumbled into the greenhouse, looked at a few mediocre plants. We checked our phones, saw there was no reception, and ran back outside in a panic.

An hour and five minutes had passed. No call. I felt numb and nauseous, and when David halfheartedly said we should just get in the car and leave, I couldn't disagree with the appeal of that thought.

But we did not leave. Instead, we sat down on a small wooden bench just outside the greenhouse. Fit blue-haired ladies in sensible shoes and stout matching shorts-and-top sets came in and out, marching around officiously and talking about what they were planting that spring. A young couple with lunchtime sandwiches sat on the bench across from us. He unwrapped and devoured his sandwich. She picked at hers.

It had been an hour and fifteen minutes. Still no call. I felt so strange, so uncomfortable in my own skin, I couldn't shake the mild sense of guilt over having held and fed the baby the night before, yet at the same time felt incredibly angry that something so dumb would make such a big impact. They had shoved the kid at us for two days, for Christ's sake! If they were going to give us the freaking kid to be ours for a lifetime, what difference did three minutes in a rocking chair make?

It felt as though my guts had been scooped out of me but were still attached and I was now waiting to see whether they would be put gently back into me (we get the kid) or hurled into the wolf den for rabid gobbling (we do not get the kid).

Finally, my phone rang. I grabbed it, my heart pounding so hard in my throat that I could barely hear my own voice.

"Hello?" I said.

"Bad news." It was Marie, the head of our adoption agency in Vermont. "She decided to keep the baby."

"What? Are you kidding?" I said, I think very loudly, but I really could not tell. Drums and cymbals and a rushing sound were swelling in my head. I think I may have started to yell, then scream, but I couldn't hear a sound.

Marie said something, sorry, blah, blah, blah, something.

"I am never doing this ever again! *Never!*" I screamed. "How could you lead us into such a stupid situation and then abandon us!? Are you people insane?"

I must have held the phone away from me and David must have taken it. I do not remember hanging up with Marie. From somewhere far away David's voice asked me if I wanted to go talk to the social worker who was still at the hospital. "Are you fucking kidding me?" I yelled. "That clueless idiot? I wouldn't trust myself in his presence—I feel like punching him in his stupid goddamn face!"

The words kept coming, joined by heaving sobs. I don't know if tears ran down my face but I think I was pacing the small cement patio near the greenhouse, wailing, screaming. The young couple looked at me with scared expressions and got up and quickly left the area. An elderly woman walked briskly towards me and said, "I'm sorry—God bless you, dear," and hurried away while making the sign of the cross.

I was waving my arms and yelling, "Goddammit, how could they be so stupid? How could this happen? How could they put us in this situation, an idiot could have seen this coming! Not again! How again? I can't believe they put us through this!"

And I'm not sure what else was coming out of my mouth, but I felt capable of ripping out someone's heart with my bare hands at that moment.

David called someone, I think his father, and we literally stumbled down the hill, out of the park, and towards the hospital. I didn't want to go near the freaking place ever again, but our car was parked there, in the one spot directly in front of the main entry door. With the baby seat installed in the back. And the diapers and formula and all that crap strewn everywhere.

I called my mom from near the parking lot. I was sobbing into the phone. "They decided to keep the baby."

"Oh my God, oh no, oh honey, oh my God, no…" I told her we

were driving somewhere, I didn't know where, but that I would let her know where I was in a day or two.

"I'm getting on the next flight," Mom said. I told her not to bother, that there was absolutely nothing she could do. But thank you.

I hung up and threw the shoes and newborn footprints and baby Yankee outfit into the nearest trash can. We stuffed the baby seat, the one we had so carefully installed, back into the trunk. David drove.

"Get us out of this fucking hellhole. And I am *not* going home." I couldn't bear the thought of a decorated crib, of welcome gifts and cards, of calls from my co-workers who knew I had been on my way to pick up my son, not to mention the heavily pregnant and unwelcome tenants downstairs. David looked at the map. Upstate New York is not exactly chock-full of great choices in terms of lovely places to emotionally convalesce.

So we headed to the only hospitable place we could find on the map between Rochester and New York City—Saratoga.

Step Away from the Clowns

WE WERE LEAVING TOWN, getting the hell out of Rochester, a name which, to this day, I cannot say without a flashback and visceral memory of the bizarre sensation of experiencing unbearable emotional anguish while being showered by the fluttering petals of inexplicably gorgeous trees; the incongruity of the two sensations reminds me of something from a bizarre old David Lynch movie. The experience practically ruined my enjoyment of blossoming cherry or lilac trees, since I still cannot yet separate that dreamily lush bit of memory from the searing emotional pain.

But we had one stop to make before we left town. A day earlier, in a fit of love and generosity, we had bought Karlie a lovely gold pendant for her birthday, which had been a few days before she delivered the baby. In my anguish, I considered throwing the jewelry into the trash, along with all the other baby paraphernalia, but even in my desperate state I hated the thought of tossing away the few hundred dollars we had spent. "Get rid of it," I muttered in David's direction.

"Do you want to...?" David began.

"Just get rid of it—get it out of here," I repeated.

We parked at the mall, David went in and I waited in the car for what felt like an eternity. I glared at the sidewalk, I seethed at the sky. I hated Rochester, every brick, every stoplight—I wanted to smash something, to blame someone. The world no longer made any sense to me whatsoever.

Finally, David reappeared with a small box in his hands. "They wouldn't give us a refund so I got you these." Inside was a pair of ruby earrings. "My birthstone," I said. I tossed the box in the backseat and asked David to floor it out of town.

This whole chapter strikes me as funny now but it was anything but in the moment; when we got to Saratoga and headed to the first major hotel we saw, we got out of the car and stumbled towards the front door, me still snuffling back tears, the anger starting to set in deep and hard. A clown—a full-on, red wig, Bozo floppy feet and big red nose clown—approached me.

"Honk, honk." He beeped his nose.

I was aghast. I do not like clowns on a good day. Bad scary, not funny, last on my list, do not like them.

I glanced at David. He didn't register. "Honey," I said with a serious glance.

"Honk, honk." The clown again.

My fists clenched.

"How about a smile, little lady?" leered the clown.

I took a halting, deliberate deep breath.

"Honey, make the clown step away from me." David stood still, looking from me to the clown, as if this were all a surreal painting.

"Honey!" David grabbed my arm and walked me towards the front door of the hotel just before I lunged for the clown's throat.

The evening was dark; the pungent springtime smell of the trees and flowers and grass and wet earth of Saratoga filled my senses. I breathed in slowly, starting to relax. Wine, I need wine, I thought. I can get through this. That was not meant to be my child—David and I both felt that. I smiled over at David, he smiled back. And then he reached for the hotel's front door.

WELCOME, NATIONAL CLOWN CONVENTION. The sign was in big red letters.

"No, no, I can't..." I said.

"Come on," David said and pulled me through the door.

If timing is everything, then I have been to Hell.

To my left was a hallway that emptied into a large room, chock-full of clowns. Big ones in red wigs with floppy shoes like our greeter outside. Little ones with bald heads and sad eyes. Male, female, old, young, gleeful, and sorry—there were more fucking clowns than I ever hoped to see.

David towed me towards the concierge desk. "I am sorry sir," the man said from underneath his red wig (I guess the Marriott prides themselves on getting into the spirit of their guests), "we have no vacancies. Convention, you know..."

"Thanks, thanks," we muttered and sprinted towards the exit.

We found the only vacant room in town at what could fairly be called the Bates Motel, a dim, animal-trophied, off-the-beaten-path kind of joint. A huge deer head faced us as we lay in the sagging bed. At around three in the morning the room shook so hard it almost tossed us out of bed, and I thought it was the subway until I remembered we weren't in the city. Oh yeah—the drive, our supposed son, the fucking lilac trees, the pain—we were in Saratoga. Apparently, there is a fault, as in earthquake fault, in that part of New York, and it had been triggered.

I like to think that the Saratoga earthquake—big enough to make the Bambi deer head nod at us but not fall from its precarious perch on the faux wood-paneled wall—was the beginning of the rearranging of my mind. I had to let go—totally, with finality—to any notion of How Things Were Going to Be. The world, my motherhood, the date it would all begin—these were clearly mysteries beyond my control. And I was simply too exhausted, utterly wrung out, to pretend to wrest control of the whole scenario.

As we returned home a few days later and I spoke to family and friends and told our adoption agency that we were never—*ever*—going to go through another situation with them, and how could they possibly have left us so alone in what was obviously a tenuous situation, it slowly began to set in with finality. I knew that I was on my own path, and that someday, through adoption, hopefully before I was drooling and in a walker, I would be somebody's mother.

Meanwhile, Back in Brooklyn

DESPITE MY BEST INTENTIONS, the Zen-like wisdom I was so smugly and briefly in possession of flew right out the window as soon as we got home and I watched the now heavily pregnant Sonya waddle out the front door of our basement apartment and hang out on the front stoop. My front stoop.

What is the last thing, I mean the very last thing I could stand at this point? What single thing would be guaranteed to send me screaming right over the edge? I asked myself in a twisted mutter.

Hmm, I answered, *I would say that it would be having to watch someone go through a blissful pregnancy right under my fucking nose. Say, in my very own house, the one place left on the planet that I can control and from which pregnant women are forbidden.*

Yes, life is often wicked, with a warped and relentless sense of humor.

We had been talking for months about telling Jason that staying in the small studio apartment wouldn't work. We had rented it to him alone, and he had since added on his girlfriend, a large, unfriendly dog (all of our neighbors hated us for that), and now an impending baby.

"Have you been around many little babies?" I had asked. "They themselves are small, but all their loot—it'll fill the entire place!"

After I suggested that we sit down and talk it through, Jason played on David's softheartedness, saying, "This is the time I need to think about my family," and, "This is our *home.*"

I wanted to scream, "It's not your home, you moron, it's *my* home! And it's a tiny studio home at that. There ain't no way a kid is gonna fit in there with y'all!"

"You know, Sonya will be so sad—maybe even depressed, if she has to leave this neighborhood," Jason said seriously of his girlfriend.

How dare he? I thought, as if I alone was standing in the way of her eternal happiness.

I looked over at David, waiting for him to rise to my defense, but he just sat there like a rock.

I felt like ripping Jason's face off; the thought of having to watch Sonya dodder around daily, sunning herself, rubbing her belly, while a steady stream of grinning friends dropped by with cutesy little gift baskets—and I couldn't even contemplate when the baby actually arrived—all of it made me want to pack a bag and run away.

Instead, I took a deep breath and steeled myself. "There are no fewer than three real estate offices on every single block around here for a mile, with literally dozens of great rental listings in each one. I'm sure you can find something perfect if you just look."

My level of anger surprised me, and I was sure I would be shot if anyone could hear my thoughts of Sonya, downstairs wafting around for the last nine months, doing her freaking aromatherapy one day a month (and him an underemployed house painter—no wonder they can't afford to move!), standing there with that dazed look on her face saying, "Oh, I got offered a job but I turned it down—I'm really enjoying just having some time right now," whilst I left the house for the office at the crack of dawn, schlepping three bags, or came back exhausted to see Sonya leaning against the stairs slowly peeling an orange while the crazy dog Jack lunged at the neighbors. "Jaaaackkkk," Sonya would smile, small children and old people on walkers trying to steer away from our yard as they shot daggers over the snarling dog in my direction. "He's really very sweet, yes he's quite gawwww-jusss." Or when something really struck her as great, she'd say, "Ohhh, blessss," with a little whinny.

Unfortunately, Jason the tenant was very cunning, the type whose worldly POV is that his own needs supersede anyone else's. David was the perfect bad combo with him, being allergic to confrontation and extremely reluctant to ever say no.

Ultimately David agreed to give them three months to find a place, and I was left feeling bereft in my own home, angst-ridden that the house we had just so painfully and extensively redone was not to be my refuge, my oasis, the one place on the planet where I did *not* have to see pregnant women or maintain composure.

Some sympathetic girlfriends offered to come over and tap dance every night until we drove out Jason and Sonya, the thought of which made me laugh so hard that I cried, and it jolted me into letting go of some of the anger I was harboring. (Some months later, after their baby was born, Jason and Sonya did finally move to a larger apartment elsewhere in the area.)

So, how to stay healthy amidst all this venting? I reminded myself of the note I sent to a friend and co-worker about the irritating but perhaps truthful Oprah-ism: "It's not a problem—it's a divine opportunity." Meaning that the difficult times are not only those that we can surprise ourselves by surviving, but that they are often the ones that are the most enlightening and thus rewarding, although usually in hindsight. I had been amazed to think that a young co-worker had considered me her positivity role model—if only she knew what horrid and hateful thoughts ran through my mind!

Desperate for a distraction, life served me up a doozy. I discovered a tiny water spot in the ceiling of our upstairs bedroom, called David (who was out of town for work, as usual), and he sent a team from his company over to fix it. Five guys in filthy boots showed up and pounded on the roof for a while, at which point I left the house for some peace and quiet. When the drizzle turned to a downpour, I ran back home to discover that not only had the workers left the house for the day, but they had apparently made a much bigger hole in the roof, so much so that the water was literally pouring through in buckets, soaking not only our room (and its new carpet), but also leaking through the beams from the top floor into the ground floor.

I called David in desperation, and the idiot workers came back in to tarp the roof. Ultimately, we ended up replacing the whole roof, and David agreed to pay more than triple the average cost. I vehemently disagreed but decided that, just like so many other things in life, I had to let it go.

To Russia with Love
(or, Did You Say Siberia?)

AND SO I TURNED MY attention fully back to gathering up all the thousands of documents needed to secure our application with our international adoption agency to go to Russia.

The list was overwhelming: birth certificates, marriage licenses, divorce decrees (ours was a second marriage for both David and me), proof of everywhere we had lived for the past twenty years, and all of it—every single page of every single document—had to be apostilled, which is like being super-notarized. It is a separate and additional step and fee to a notary, and has to go through a particular and specific office depending on what state you are in.

To add even more fun to the amount of pleading phone calls and scurrying all over town I did every day, standing in line at various government offices with hours-long lines of people requesting all manner of obscure documentation, the agency demanded that all the documents be originals, even if that meant writing letters to states where we were born and speaking to what sounded like toothless, semi-retired janitors filling in for frazzled, resigned bureaucrats who were constantly unavailable.

I would call up an office (say for our birth certificates), which often required days of phone calls referring me to other offices in a scenario something like the following—I would call the city where said event took place, they would refer me to the Secretary of State, I would leave three unreturned messages, then finally reach someone named Moon Sunshine (only in California) who would dig through drawers full of pre-computer carbon copies and then refer me back to the city office that had referred me to her in the first place.

I would then call back to the office I had started with, and after a week of leaving messages, would finally reach someone who told me in a sleepy voice, "Those records are too old—they wouldn't be here anymore—they've been sent downtown."

"Where downtown?" I would ask.

"South Central."

"South Central what? Can you, uh, can you tell me where to call?"

"Call South Central."

I would realize that I was clenching and unclenching my fists and moving my feet back and forth under my desk as though I was running in place.

Remember to breathe, I would think. This is all part of the process, part of my path. Part of my beautiful, inevitable fucking path.

"Great, thanks. Can you give me the phone number?" I would smile, hoping it translated into my voice, which would translate into this faceless person taking it upon themselves to help me.

I would get the number, take a deep breath, and punch it in, then wait while the phone rang endlessly on the other side of the country. I would be close to hanging up when a voice came slowly into my ear.

"'Lo." The voice was definitely male, definitely old, and definitely from the Deep South.

I explained what I was after.

"I dunno, ma'am, I'm just here answerin' the phone for a minute, I usually just sweep up and stuff..."

The sweet old man made it clear that I needed to call back when the office staff was in. He also made it clear that he was not at all certain when that might be.

This type of process was the norm, but slowly I started to accumulate a giant pile of the necessary documents. If it blew over, I imagined it would create a paper blizzard akin to the blizzards they must have in Russia. I definitely had Russia on the mind...

The summer crept by, my stack of paperwork grew, and finally, in late August, I was able to deliver our completed dossier to the agency.

"You can expect to get a referral [detailed information about our prospective child] in one to four months," I was told. "You can expect to take two trips to Russia—during the first trip, you will meet your child. Then you will come back home and wait for a court date, at which time you fly back, go to court, officially adopt the child, and then fly home."

"Great!" I said. "But why can't we meet the child and bring her home all in one trip? What is the point of waiting?"

The agency did not have a great response, but simply chalked it up to Russian bureaucracy, and then admitted that it was likely simply due to the government's desire to wring more money out of the whole adoption process.

I was living on the edge of my seat and every single time the phone rang—at work, at home, or on my mobile—my heart pounded and I thought, "Maybe it's them, maybe it's finally our baby!"

As we got ready to leave for summer vacation, the agency said, "Your dossier has been sent to Russia, everything was in order..." *Hallelujah!* I thought—*after all the time-consuming, crazy-making legwork and expense of this ordeal, everything is in order!*

"It has?" I said gleefully. "It's been sent to Russia?"

"Yes. You're going to...let me see what region they've sent you to..."

I tried to breathe casually, as though my entire future, my child, my family, did not hang in this one little balance. I imagined the elegant turrets of Moscow, the sophistication of St. Petersburg, of snow-capped domes and full cafes of locals sipping vodka and espresso.

I held my breath.

"Kemerovo. They've sent your dossier to Kemerovo. Novokuznetsk."

"That's great! Kemerovo Novokuts... What did you call it? Is that near Moscow? Where's Kemerovo?" I asked.

"Siberia."

Had I heard that right? Did he just say Siberia?

"Ha ha, that's funny—it sounded like you said Siberia!" I laughed. Silence on the other end.

"Hello?" I stammered.

"We do a lot of adoptions in Siberia," the agency man said dryly.

"Really? Siberia!" I tried to sound excited, like Siberia was just A-okay with me, but my mind was reeling, my heart pounding. *"Siberia?"* I wanted to yell. *"Well, that makes perfect freaking sense! Of course, we wouldn't be sent to St. Petersburg in the springtime, no—of course, after the hell of the last four years, what else could make sense but that we would pay $30,000 to go to Siberia in the dead of winter!"*

"Woowwwww, that sounds great..." I said lamely. "Siberia is a place I have always wondered about..." Bald-faced lie.

The agency went on to tell me that they had been placing a lot of children from Kemerovo, that they'd been mainly healthy, and when I asked for phone numbers of people who'd adopted from there, they happily complied.

I hung up dazed, the image of me standing in a snowstorm bundled from head to toe, a dog sled next to me, while two arms poked out of an igloo holding a squalling, mummy-wrapped tiny package of a baby.

Still, many of the finest minds in Russia had been sent to Siberia during the Stalinist era. Writers, poets, philosophers, politicians, teachers—many were sent to the frozen north, and if the research I began doing was true, more than seventy percent of the population in Kemerovo had college and/or graduate degrees. There was hope!

The Waiting

I HAD DELIVERED OUR DOSSIER to our international adoption agency in late August. Huzzah! Given that they said our travel date was to be in one to three months, four maximum from dossier delivery date, I was positive that we'd be jetting off to the motherland—Russia, specifically Siberia—any week now. I let my mind be voraciously optimistic and imagined that I might even have my first Thanksgiving as a mother. Certainly by Christmas…well, let's be reasonable, I told myself—we will positively have taken our first trip by the end of the year, but perhaps we won't be back with our daughter before the new year.

Novokuznetsk is in the region of Kemerovo in southwestern Siberia and is the second-largest city after Kemerovo, with a population of a little over half a million people. When I looked it up, I discovered that Novokuznetsk had been founded in 1618 by men from Tomsk as a Cossack fort. It was in fact where Fyodor Dostoevsky married his first wife, Maria Isaeva, in 1857. Under Stalin's fast industrialization, it became a coal mining and industrial hub in the 1930s.

Okay, I thought—if it's good enough for Dostoevsky, it's good enough for me!

What about the weather? I imagined white and snow and more white as far as the eye can see. It turns out that the area has a pretty typical Siberian climate, which is to say cold, with frequent but dry snowfall in the winter due to the very cold temperatures. How cold is cold, I wondered? After all, I was by that point a seasoned New Yorker, and a little snow and sleet didn't faze me.

It looked like the average daily temperature was about twenty degrees, with snow likely during the time we would be there. Okay, not too bad, not ten below or anything! I figured the down coat I had would do the trick and keep me toasty.

It looked like the region was home to at least a half-dozen major universities of medical and other sciences, as well as almost as many heavy industrial facilities like steel and aluminum factories. I expected extremely well-educated people living in a post-industrial and heavily polluted snowy land.

And so we waited. September went by (that was one month), then October (two months). I went out and bought a *better*, longer down coat, thinking, "It's definitely going to be November, it's going to be twenty below…" I said to myself too many times, "As long as we're out of town for November, that's all I want…" meaning, "Please, let us get to freaking Siberia before I have to face another freaking childless holiday season!"

October passed and November rolled in (month three—when were they going to call?). Dreaded Thanksgiving loomed—what had once been my due date (the ectopic pregnancy), then an adoption due date…not my favorite month.

Then I got it into my mind that I would get the call with a referral by the first half of December. The agency did not discourage my hope on my occasional phone calls. "Just checking in," I would say as brightly as I could.

But the days and then weeks rolled by with no phone calls or babies to report, and another new year stared me in the face.

I knew what was coming—another holiday season filled with a barrage of holiday cards with kiddies stuffed into giant stockings at the local family photo shop, of pictures of young adults, children of people I knew before they had even met their current spouses and who were now seriously married and gaily sending off souvenirs of their domestic bliss at every given holiday.

Still, the thought of perhaps having my own child, a little girl, to cuddle and dress up and *ooh* and *aah* over would change every aspect of the holiday season. So I celebrated the end of another year and rang in the new one with hopes—no, certainty!—that the next year would be the one in which I became a mother.

But still I couldn't help but pace and fret—why was it taking so long for us to get a referral and travel date? It was going on four-plus months since I had delivered the dossier. I had images of a sultry blond in a crooked fedora delivering a swath of papers to a tall, dangerous Russian in a dark alley, or perhaps over a shot of vodka in an after-hours nightclub. Being of Russian descent myself—a happy coincidence, I would've taken a child from any country—I felt a sense of proprietary pride about all things Russian and was very much looking forward to going and seeing the country from which my namesake maternal grandmother had sailed before landing on the shores of Chicago sometime in the early 1900s.

Meanwhile, we in America endured a crazy and rigged presidential election, and in the State of the Union address, I watched in disbelief as "President" George W. Bush moved to cut taxes for the wealthiest people in the country, who were some of the wealthiest in the world; with his incendiary and blustery language, I prayed that he wouldn't reignite the Cold War, at least not before we had a chance to get to Russia and pick up our daughter.

But I also had some wonderful distractions; my two great girl-friends—the same ones who had merrily threatened to tap dance our idiotic and selfish downstairs tenants out of our home—threw me a hilarious vodka-and-caviar-infused, Russian-themed bon voyage, complete with fur hats, beautiful Russian children's books, and lots of laughter.

And then one day at work, seemingly out of the blue—I got the call. "You are scheduled to meet a little girl on March 17, so you will travel..." The voice on the phone faded quickly to in indistinct drone, like the parents' voices in the old Peanuts cartoons. "Wah wah wah wah wah wah wah..."

We were going to *Russia*! I was going to meet my *daughter*! I was finally—unbelievably—going to become a *mother*!

The voice on the phone blurted out travel dates. We were to fly out of JFK on March 15 at 6 P.M. and arrive in Moscow the next morning at 11 A.M. (they are eight hours ahead). We would stay in Moscow for a few hours, then fly out that same night for Siberia, where we would arrive early the following morning.

We were scheduled to return to NYC on March 21, having met our daughter. Hooray!

As my heart pounded and my mind reeled, giddy with excitement and literally spinning in circles, I made sure I had my book list: *The Russian Adoption Handbook, Raising Adopted Children, The Parents' Guide to Adopted Children.*

My heart was beating so hard I thought it would burst right out of my body. I checked the calendar—we were to fly to Russia for our first trip in only two weeks!

I went over my notes for the nintieth time; I needed to make sure to get all the medical information and reports from the orphanage, which would likely have a dedicated doctor. I was excited already and imagined how hard it would be to keep my wits about me when we actually, finally, met our daughter!

I thought it best if I wrote down all the questions to ask at the orphanage.

My protocol with our consulting pediatrician Dr. Jane Aronson would be:

- We would gather all the info, pictures, and ideally video of the child in question and send it to her via fax at the end of our day Russia time. (Cell phones were less reliable back then, and who knew how it might be from Siberia?)
- We would call to confirm that they received all the information.
- When they get all the documents, Dr. Aronson's assistant gives us a time slot to call the doctor.
- When we spoke to Dr. Aronson, she would give us a risk assessment (low, medium, or high) and comment on the child's growth chart.
- We would try to get a four- to five-minute video of each possible child.

- We should record the doctor's answers to our questions (in the orphanage).

And in terms of the records about the baby:
- Birth weight
- Growth charts
- Head circumference
- Apgar scores (a test performed right after birth)
- Vaccination records
- Any illnesses in the orphanage

Last but not least, I checked for the third time that I had our giant stack of documents: our dossier, three copies of our passports, our visas and copies of same, $3,500 in new U.S. dollars, the video camera and tape recorder, and the book of pictures (our house, neighborhood, parks, etc.).

I was so excited that I could not help but look at the list for trip number 2, when we would get to actually bring our daughter home! I was already running through the list in my mind—I would need to bring bottles and nipples, a pacifier, baby clothes, the pediatrician's letter, our acceptance form, etc.

I looked again at the list of possible names, knowing that I'd have to see her face before I would know which name would best suit her: Ava Gabrielle (or Gabrielle Ava), Grace, Isabel, Hope, Antonia. And what about boys' names, just for the heck of it? Hmmm—how about Stefan Chandler, Sergei, Sasha, Sebastian or Spencer?

Hmmmm... My mind reeled with excitement, anticipation, disbelief. This was going to be *amazing*.

II. Russia

Siberia or Bust

Early March

AFTER PACKING, UNPACKING, and repacking numerous times (chalk it up to nerves), I finally had my suitcase ready to roll. JFK Airport overnight to Moscow, then Moscow overnight to Siberia. Wow.

Some friends toasted us with champagne and caviar (everyone knew I loved caviar and how Russian a tradition it is), and off to JFK we went.

A representative from our adoption agency told me that we'd be picked up at the airport in Moscow and either taken to another airport to leave for Siberia or have some time to look around the great city of Moscow. The truth was, as soon as we boarded the eight-or-so-hour Delta Airlines flight to Moscow, we were in the hands of our agency and, more importantly, their Russian counterparts.

In the cab, I checked my money and document belt yet again—I was carrying a wad of American cash (new, unwrinkled bills only, as instructed by our agency), though we had been advised that we would bring the larger "gift" of a few thousand dollars cash on the second trip and the agency would pay it out, once our adoption was complete. This was presumably so the handing over of this amount of cash would seem more like an actual *gift*—the adoption would have been "completed" so no baby-buying here—rather than a bribe. Right...

We took off, the plane full, including other families flying to meet their soon-to-be Russian adoptee children.

I gazed out the window fitfully, my emotions a mixture of excitement, trepidation, and curiosity—we had virtually no idea how this adventure might go despite the many assurances from our adoption agency. "We've done thousands of adoptions from Russia, you're in good hands," they had said. Still, after all the misadventures of the last four or so years, when someone told me there was nothing to worry about, I got distinctly worried.

A friend had given us some mild sleeping pills (I wanted to be conscious during this big event) and I swallowed one as I gazed out the window, New York City receding into the background.

I awoke hours later feeling refreshed and to the news that we were close to landing in Moscow. I straightened my hair, put on some lipstick, and wondered what my little girl was doing at that moment. I was a bit loopy but excited.

Two interpreters from our agency—both gorgeous young women; the Beatles weren't kidding when they said, "You don't know how lucky you are, boy" in their song "Back in the USSR"—met us at the Moscow airport. We had left NYC at six P.M., and it was now almost noon Moscow time. We had a nice lunch with the women and enjoyed pierogis, meats, fish, and caviar, all very blue-collar stuff in Moscow, all of the food delicious. The restaurant was a large Russian country-themed place, made to look like a huge rustic log cabin but with a serious-faced, furry-hatted, faux guard out front. Woven blankets, wooden instruments, and tapestries covered every wall.

During our short stopover in Moscow, we saw Red Square, the Kremlin, and the old KGB building. It was a clear, beautiful, cold day, and the city was fascinating looking, full of history and unique turreted buildings. The majority of people on the street looked familiar to me—I thought I saw my mother more than once—and I was acutely aware of my own Russian heritage.

I was rather bleary by the afternoon, having left our house yesterday at noon NYC time, so I was hoping to sleep en route to Siberia. We were due to arrive in Siberia at 4:30 A.M. (with Siberia being exactly twelve hours ahead of NYC) their time and the next day we would meet our prospective daughter. I wanted to be rested enough to at least be able to see straight.

But before we headed back to the airport, we were driven around and offered the chance to buy some mementoes and touristy trinkets in Red Square—the little wooden nesting dolls, where the large one holds a smaller one, holds a smaller one, and so on. We declined but ended up in a more private (and expensive) shop where David was convinced to spend $400 on what would have cost $25 in Red Square. Four hundred American dollars was more than some Russians made in a year, and I was nudging him to put items down and be more reasonable. But the truth was, I wasn't into fighting over the small stuff at this point—we were about to meet our daughter!

In hindsight, I am certain that the agency and the various businesses had some sort of monetary arrangement, and that every business our agency hosts took us into had some sort of "agreement" involving kickbacks. I get it, people need to make money and here come some "rich" Americans with cash to spare. Everyone needs to maximize opportunity to survive, but there was not even much of an attempt to pretend otherwise, which I found surprising. Corruption, pay-offs, "favors," whatever you wanted to call it, this type of arrangement and/or payback seemed to permeate every aspect of Russian life as far as visiting Americans were concerned, and everyone we met seemed very comfortable with the overt nature of the monetary "gifts" to be exchanged. Little did I know how much more extreme the situation was going to become.

Later I found out that many locals say, "There is Moscow and then there is Russia," meaning the average worker in Russia at that point made the equivalent of about twenty dollars a month (including doctors and taxi drivers, who were roughly in the same income bracket) so we had just spent more than a year's income on trinkets.

Sigh. I chalked it up to excitement and exhaustion and on we went, my thoughts turning to our next flight, which would take us overnight to Siberia.

It was March 16, a Sunday, and we were heading back to the airport to board a plane to Novokuznetsk, Siberia.

Thank goodness our Moscow translator/hostess saw us to and through the airport; the Moscow airport was clean and tidy but very crowded with officious and impatient, scowling people, none of whom seemed to ever smile or speak English (not to sound imperialist—why would they speak English?). But with our translator's help we got through all the checkpoints we needed to and were about to wander off for drinks and snacks when we were told we needed to board. We crammed onto a bus, then were driven out onto the tarmac where we milled like cattle being squeezed through a chute at the bottom of the stairs that lead to the plane. It was like NYC in rush hour—lots of shoving, very little space.

When I got enough room to breathe, I looked up at the plane we were to board for the overnight flight to Siberia. It looked like a recycled WWII fighter, everything faded and rusted, the once-shiny silver metal covered in duct tape, the entire outline of the doorway and many of the windows on the side heavy with the silver tape.

Now, I have a theory that you can fix anything with duct tape, but flying in the dark through sub-zero degrees across the frozen Russian tundra for hours on end, relying on an antique plane and many rolls of duct tape to secure our passage, I must admit I was skeptical.

But then the bear-sized guy behind me gave me a little shove and mumbled something in Russian, and next thing I knew I had walked carefully up the frozen metal stairs (very Jackie O) and found my way down the cramped aisle and into a tiny seat.

The seats were impossibly small, and a very large man, well over six feet tall and meaty, was squeezed in on my left, his body pinching out over the seat in every direction. I nodded hello and smiled. He nodded back, no smile. How very Russian.

There was not one square inch left unfilled on the plane. And everything was heavy. And metal. The tray tables were metal, and when you unhooked them, their weight brought them crashing down to the open position. Heavy metal, I thought sarcastically, as a Muzak version of Pink Floyd's "Us and Them" blasted out. It was a nearly full moon on a crisp and cloudless night. I hoped for a smooth flight, and figured that if this cobbled-together, ex–fighter jet full of heavy metal could make it off the ground, it might be as smooth as flying a '68 Cadillac.

It's a good thing that Russia is so huge, because that Siberian-bound plane seemed to roll down that runway forever, though when it finally—thankfully, I breathed a sigh and realized I had been holding my breath—got off the ground, neither snow nor hail nor gusts of icy wind could buffet it, and we rolled on into the freezing Russian night as though we were on a 150,000-pound couch.

The food on the flight was very good—real meat of course (only twelve hours into our Russian adventure, I had already learned that a meal was not considered a real meal, especially to a Russian man, without meat), beet salad, some other very tasty sides, likely some fish. It was dark outside so there was no land to look down on, only hours and hours of invisible acreage as we headed farther away from Moscow and closer to the Chinese border. I think I slept fitfully, then awoke when we were gliding down through some turbulence.

Siberia—we had arrived! I could hardly believe it! After all the years—the pregnancies, the in vitro and travel and shots, the domestic adoption debacles, the hell of Rochester—finally, here I was, landing on the other side of the planet, about to meet my daughter.

Siberian Gray

WHEN THE PLANE DOORS opened and we made our way down the frozen metal stairway and stepped out onto the tarmac, it certainly looked like we were in Novokuznetsk, Siberia. There was snow to the left. Snow to the right. Giant piles of frozen snow framed every line around the airport and runway, all of it stained a dingy gray, presumably from the unceasing spewing of industrial pollutants. There was nothing to break the sight of endless, flat gray in all directions—no mountains, no tall buildings, nothing much on the landscape but endless gray and off-white, frozen mounds of icy snow in every direction.

We were met on the tarmac at the small airport by a local interpreter, Natasha, and our RAA local rep, also named Natasha. But as would become increasingly clear with each passing moment, the two Natashas could not have been more different. Interpreter Natasha (or Nice Natasha, as I would come to call her) was bright and smiling, with long light-brown hair; she spoke four or five languages fluently and held three advanced degrees. It's true what they say about Siberia, I thought—so many brainy Russians ended up here! She was helpful and sweet and had kind eyes.

Natasha Number 2, our agency rep (aka Scary Natasha), was her polar opposite. Everything about Scary Natasha was dark and ominous; she was short and wide and stern, with mean dark eyes and long, obviously dyed jet-black-blue hair. She wore a constant scowl and looked disdainfully at me from the moment she laid eyes on me. This demeanor never let up and when she did have to speak to me through Nice Natasha, Scary Natasha literally hissed her angry words out in my direction.

Scary Natasha wore overtly expensive-looking, gaudy clothes—a fur coat, skintight leather pants, oversized gold-nugget jewelry, very high, metal-studded boots—and full, stage-strength makeup, even at 4 A.M. when we first met her on the tarmac as we landed in Siberia. I think I whispered "dominatrix" to David when I first saw her and we giggled later, comparing her to the comically stern late, great Cloris Leachman character in *Young Frankenstein*, where every time someone said her name the horses would rear up, thunder and lightning would roar, and you'd hear "Frau Blücher!"

We were driven to the hotel in a small generic car—all of the cars we rode in were very small by American standards—by a handsome driver who looked like a younger, larger, and angrier Kris Kristofferson. Unfortunately, he was of a temperament similar to Scary Natasha's, his large unsmiling face glaring disapprovingly at me in the rearview mirror as we drove. Maybe this was their schtick, to play mean cop roles and intimidate "wealthy" want-to-be adoptive parents who'd traveled across the world, but when he and Scary Natasha muttered to each other during the drive, I was pretty sure they were planning to drive us out to some gulag and dump us there. To say I felt unwelcome would be an understatement.

After passing lots of half-finished buildings—it looked like parts of old Baja California, where luxury resorts were left half-built and then abandoned after investors bailed or ran out of money—we arrived at a large, generic-looking hotel. Before we could check in, we were ushered to a desk where they took our passports. "Excuse me," I smiled, "I'd like to hold on to my passport please." I already felt vulnerable enough, being surrounded by people who were supposed to be on our team but who obviously disapproved of us. Heartily.

The woman behind the desk, unsmiling with a world-weary expression (it is a running joke even amongst Russians themselves that they are famous for never smiling), snapped something back at me and Nice Natasha, our always-smiling interpreter, said, "She say no, you must give them passport to hold while you stay here, they give back when it is time for you to leave." We had no choice, apparently, so the unsmiling woman behind the hotel desk held on to our passports.

"Stranded in Siberia" ran vaguely through my sleepless mind as we found our way to our room, which was very small and held two tiny, sagging cots, something like the mother's bed in *Psycho*, where her body had lain there so long that the deep indentation down the center of the bed was permanent.

We were excited, exhausted, full of anticipation; I was giddy imagining the moment of meeting, holding, smelling, feeling my daughter. At the same time, it had been such a long, sometimes absurd, often unreal and painstaking journey, capped off by these last two overnight plane trips in a row, that some part of my bedraggled mind would not let me believe it until I saw it.

We put down our bags and returned to the lobby as instructed, eager to go to the orphanage where we would finally meet our little girl.

It was Monday, March 17, early afternoon Siberia time. I couldn't help but think that this date, this time, this exact place and moment, would later be indelibly etched in my heart as the Beginning.

I was almost queasy with anticipation and excitement.

Orphanage Number 1

WE WERE DRIVEN to the orphanage by the Natashas and the scowling Kris Kristofferson. A number of other couples who had flown in to meet their soon-to-be adoptive children were going to see their children as well, so the mood was exhausted but full of giddy optimism.

We arrived at a modest, cold-looking gray cement building that we were told was Orphanage Number 1, where we were to meet our daughter. After stiff introductions to the orphanage staff, all done via Nice Natasha and her reassuring smile, we were ushered into a small private room, the orphanage doctor's office, where the doctor began to rattle off statistics that Nice Natasha relayed to me in English. The length of the pregnancy, the child's head circumference at birth, etc., all recited by the orphanage doctor, a young woman, stern and unsmiling.

The orphanage doctor said something and paused for Nice Natasha's translation. "She was born in March of 2000..." and on she went.

What, I thought? Can that be right? That would make this little girl three years old, definitely not five months old as we had been told.

"Excuse me," I said softly. "This little girl..."

"Iliana, she is called Iliana," Nice Natasha said.

"If I understand correctly, Iliana is three years old, and while she sounds lovely, we were expecting, we were told that we would be meeting a more or less six-month-old girl. A baby…"

David sank down in his chair. The couple leaning in the doorway, who were adopting preteen siblings and had merrily met them already, looked at me with a sorrowful, apologetic expression.

Scary Natasha was whispering to the orphanage director, who was looking back and forth between Nice Natasha and me.

I looked at Nice Natasha, who seemed our only ally. "We were told we were meeting a little girl, about six months old, and that is our wish and dream and what we are prepared for…" I tried to explain, aware that I didn't want to come off like a spoiled American, which I was certain was the way they saw us, or to be insensitive to the poor little girl Iliana.

Scary Natasha said something that sounded very stern and final and the orphanage doctor continued, translated by Nice Natasha.

With her sunshiny smile still intact, Nice Natasha said, "And so Iliana has been in this orphanage first when she was four months, then again when she was one and one-half years, again at two years, and again now…"

"Wait, what? What do you mean?" I asked, more confused than ever.

"You see," Nice Natasha continued, "it is quite frequent for Russian women, young mothers, when can't feed their children that they bring to orphanage, then they come pick them up to go home when they again have money or job or if father comes back…"

Poor little Iliana sounded mainly physically healthy though her mother sounded like she couldn't afford to feed her so kept bringing her back there, then picking her up, then bringing her back, something I later found out had happened to my mother as child when her Russian immigrant mother lived in Chicago. But as the orphanage doctor rattled off statistics for Nice Natasha to repeat to us—Apgar score, birth weight, the inoculations she'd had, her social habits—my heart was feeling, *This is not my daughter.* And I did not like the feeling of our "hosts" trying to pull one over on us by presenting us with a very different child and scenario than the one we had been promised.

I was in a dilemma.

They refused to let us leave without at least meeting the poor girl. "Wouldn't that just be cruel and confusing for her?" I asked, but off they trundled us, David angrily silent, obviously hating every second but unwilling to speak up.

I bantered back and forth but it became clear that they were not going to let us leave the orphanage without meeting this poor little abandoned girl.

I looked over at David—his mouth was clamped shut, tight and straight as a line in a cartoon drawing.

"Excuse me," I said, "I am sure she is a beautiful child, and she deserves a forever family, but we are looking to adopt a child as young as possible. As you have probably seen from our dossier, we have been trying to become parents for quite a long time, and the longer a child is in an orphanage the more likely that…"

Scary Natasha said something loud and fast in Russian, cutting me off. Nice Natasha sunnily smiled, "You will meet her."

Even though I was jet-lagged, sleepless, and stuck in Siberia with no passport, standing next to a miserable, mute husband and clearly at the apparent mercy of some locals who held me in unmasked disdain, I could see what Scary Natasha was up to; her whole game was to intimidate and bully, probably share some of our American cash and gifts with her circle of cronies, and she was obviously a master at manipulating and controlling the scenario.

"No," I said, "I mean, won't that be confusing for her? We are not her forever family…" No one responded; David sat frozen. Scary Natasha stood up and everyone stood after her as if they were following an army general and we slowly filed out of the tiny room and down a long, industrial-looking hallway, passed closed doors that I imagined had bassinets full of babies and kids behind them.

We were ushered into a private room with play toys scattered around and one wall of tall windows facing the hallway from which we had just come. It had the effect of making me feel like a lizard on display in a terrarium.

Poor little Iliana; she was a wan, pale, frail little thing, and she looked both physically and emotionally malnourished. In a word, limp. We pretended to play—we didn't understand a word of each other's language—and I felt like we were a couple of trained seals. Iliana looked exhausted and confused and I imagined that all she really wanted in the whole world was to see her mother walk through the door and take her away, away to wherever home might be.

The Natashas and the rest of the adoption folks, the orphanage director and doctor and some of the other adoptive parents-to-be, stood outside the playroom staring at us through the large windows. Every minute seemed like an hour.

Finally, someone opened the door and we were allowed to leave, and Iliana was ushered back down the hallway and behind a closed door. (We were never allowed in any orphanage to see where any of the children ate or slept or actually lived.)

Scary Natasha scowled and spit out words which Nice Natasha obediently relayed to us; we would go later to Orphanage Number 2 to see if there were any younger babies there. When I asked about the six-month-old girl we had been told we were going to meet, we got no answer.

Somehow we made it back through the snow- and soot-covered streets to the hotel amidst the condolences and apologies of our fellow American adoptive parents.

Back at the hotel, all the other happy families hurried off to the ground-level hotel "office," where you could rent a computer and fax/email any information reliably back to the States since cell phone reception was at that point mostly nonexistent. I assumed they were all eager to share the happy news and photos of their new family members.

We went up to our depressing room where David went to sleep and I paced the floor, gazing out at the gray expanse that stretched in all directions, as far as the eye could see.

No Healthy Babies

LATER THAT AFTERNOON, after the huge letdown of not meeting our daughter and realizing that we were totally at the mercy of the apparently corrupt and heartless local agency rep Scary Natasha—not to mention my heart breaking for the poor little abandoned Iliana—out of the blue there was a loud banging on our hotel room door.

I had been pacing, David sleeping. I opened the door to find both Scary and Nice Natashas standing there. Without either of us saying a word, Scary Natasha shoved her way past me and into our small, dank room, then made a show of placing a few loud and hurried phone calls with Nice Natasha standing dutifully beside her, still smiling.

After thirty minutes or so, we piled downstairs, apparently being taken to see another child in Orphanage Number 2. I wondered—is this like buying a car here; they can simply make a phone call to line up another one for us to see?

I kept asking how old this child was we were going to see. The interpreter basically ignored me until finally Scary Natasha snapped something at her and Nice Natasha told me that this next girl was five months old. *Hmph,* I thought, *we shall see.*

We arrived at Orphanage Number 2, another generic and soulless looking square cement building, and quickly spoke to a stern orphanage director who read us the medical records (at five P.M. it was after hours so no doctor was there). The five-month-old baby girl's name was Sasha. Other than that, the medical records were vague; the mother was forty years old, had not had any prenatal care, was of unknown background, and no Birth Father was mentioned.

Oh shit, I thought.

They said she had been a full-term baby but that she was small and underdeveloped probably due to her mother's malnutrition, and also that her genitalia were "underdeveloped" but that she would grow out of it.

"Genitalia underdeveloped?" I asked. "What does that mean?" Fetal alcohol syndrome, I thought. I had done plenty of research before our trip to have a general familiarity with some of the more common birth defects and I knew that "mixed" genitalia could be a symptom of it.

We saw the girl, tiny Sasha, who looked shockingly more like a tiny, sickly primate than a human; her arms were as thin and hairless as chicken wings, bent and frozen in ninety-degree angles. Her face was stuck in an awkward sideways grimace as though she would be letting out a long, angst-filled wail if she could make any sound, and her eyes bulged weirdly from her skeletal face.

"Oh my God," I muttered without thinking and stifled a sob. Scary Natasha was literally blocking the hallway that led out of the orphanage and so once again we went through the pathetic and heartbreaking charade of "playing" with this barely alive girl, all while being glared at from behind a glass wall by a cluster of unsmiling, mumbling Russian women.

I could only imagine what they were saying.

When the *babushka* came to take the poor little girl back to wherever she normally stayed, the *babushka* said, "She a beautiful Russian girl." Alas, no, I thought. Scary Natasha proclaimed to us on the drive back to the hotel that we were to meet her the next morning to go to officially adopt this "perfect, beautiful Russian girl."

The next morning, a Tuesday, we officially said no to becoming Sasha's parents.

Dr. Aronson had said what I had expected after reading the details I had dutifully jotted down and faxed to her the previous night: "Fetal alcohol syndrome, at least, likely a short lifetime of constant medical needs, extremely high risk. Extremely." And, "Her head circumference is abysmal, it should be at least thirty-two centimeters at birth and at least thirty-nine to forty centimeters by five months." She didn't want to hear anything further, saying, "It's all about the brain," and implying that brain damage was a very high possibility. (Poor little Sasha's head circumference in centimeters was in the twenties and should have been well into the forties by five months old.)

When I relayed this to the Natashas in the lobby, Scary Natasha spit out the words that Nice Natasha relayed with her usual sunny demeanor: "The Russian doctors say she is fine. Your American doctor don't know, she not here."

I smiled. "I understand but this is the doctor who will be treating the baby and we are listening to her expertise."

The lecture continued, snarling Natasha looking comical as she spat in our direction, sweet Natasha smiling through every syllable. "You Americans think you know everything, you expect it to be perfect fat Gerber baby, you not know everything," etc., etc.

When Scary Natasha finished venting and Nice Natasha fell silent, Scary Natasha insisted we go back to the first orphanage, where we had met three-year-old Iliana. I dreaded going back through those doors! What other unwelcome surprises were they going to pull on us?

"You bring gifts," Scary Natasha muttered, as though we had to make amends for not taking the first child they offered us. So we stopped en route at a tiny Russian bodega and bought chocolates and coffee as instructed like good little soldiers and then upon arrival handed them to the women who greeted us back at the dank, cold, depressing orphanage.

If Charles Dickens had imagined a bleak and sad orphanage in the heart of frozen Siberia, this was it—the smell of old oatmeal and sour milk permeated the air, there was an asylum-type hush, and a general pall hung over everything.

I actually felt okay though, having slept for the first time in days—what a difference a little shut-eye makes! It had been painful to watch the other American couples meet their children, send off their thrilled announcements and photos, and then leave to return home, and we were still there in Siberia, begging and pleading for the chance to meet an even halfway-healthy child.

So we—well, I—hatched a plan: Wait for another referral, preferably a young girl, give it another two days and if that didn't pan out, go to another region of Russia.

But first we had to get through our current visit. Once again, we sat in a cramped room with the orphanage doctor, who began rattling off facts: This little girl was named Erin, her head circumference at birth was tiny, and even then at five months old was still dangerously small. Nonetheless, I jotted down all the information so I could dutifully send it back to Dr. Aronson for her official insight, although it was clear to everyone present that this child was drastically unwell; after pretending to play and engage with the clearly unwell, motionless little Erin until they let us leave the orphanage, when we ended up back at our hotel afterwards, no one even bothered to say "beautiful Russian girl."

David was absolutely wilted and made it clear that he was eager to leave, to leave Siberia, leave Russia, leave the whole continent. I too was deflated, appalled by the treatment we were getting and heartbroken, sick to my soul, at the state of some of the children we were seeing. If these were the "healthy babies" that they showed prospective adoptive parents, in what kind of health were those poor babies we weren't allowed to see?

That evening, back in our droopy and ripe-smelling hotel room, the Natashas once again knocked on the door, came brusquely inside, conferred for a few minutes, and then turned to us.

Outside the windows the evening sky was gray, the snow in all directions was streaked gray with soot, and my mood was gray.

Nice Natasha spoke up. "She say, 'What about a boy?'"

The room went very still.

My heart sank, my jaw went slack. My mind was reeling—after so many disappointments, and then after months of planning for a girl, of imagining a daughter, picking names, planning a baby shower, imagining her face gazing up at me, of buying little dresses, of living with an image of a girl in my baby-starved mind—it was like asking a fast-moving freight train to stop on a dime and make a U-turn. And that was precisely what I was asking my heart to do.

"It is just not possible here, a girl," they told us. "Russian families take the good girls, with blue eyes; you will get boy."

"But we told them a full year ago we were looking to adopt a baby girl, as young as possible," I said to deaf ears. "It was in our numerous dossiers, on every piece of the 10,000 papers we signed, written in ink and signed many times!" My voice was rising; I was controlled but could feel a potential hysteria rising inside me.

The Natashas were standing awkwardly in our tiny hotel room, David and I conferring privately in the tiny bathroom. David said he didn't care that much, boy or girl, he just wanted to get out of there. And I genuinely didn't care if it was a boy or a girl either, but the dream of a little girl that I had seared into my heart and mind had been the one thing pulling me forward all these months, the image placating me during bouts of anger at the world and at the unfairness of the situation, and I was reluctant to let it go and not have anything in its place on which I could hang my hopes and my heart.

But that was that, I thought as we stood in the bathroom the size of an average shower stall, David and I nose to nose, the room too small for us to even close the door. It was quite clear that we would be lucky to get our passports back, much less a healthy kid, much less—the audacity!—expect the baby girl we were told we were flying literally halfway around the planet to meet.

And so a boy it was to be. As we drove back to Orphanage Number 2 where we were to meet a baby boy, I imagined a boy, a feisty and cute kid, a tiny face, a shiny new bike under a Christmas tree. My mind and heart were so hungry, if you gave me even one small hint I was off to the races imagining all the happy moments of parenthood-to-be.

Back to Orphanage Number 2 we went and that is where we met—and I fell in love with—little Fyodor.

Fyodor was born on June 21, 2002, and his mother had abandoned him in a maternity hospital. It had been her second pregnancy, her first delivery (you can read between the lines). More details, all scribbled carefully down by me, and then the biggie—his Apgar score at birth. "Oh, we don't have that," the doctor said. A likely story, I thought, and a sure danger sign.

"We did do an ultrasonic on his brain which is normal for his length of premature," the doctor added through our interpreter.

What the hell did that mean?

"Since he was premature, he was in a special department in the hospital."

I wondered what they weren't telling us, and my heart sank as once again I thought, here comes another incredibly unwell, permanently unhealthy baby. "There was no pathology found," the doctor continued. Her words were meaningless, medically and emotionally. I felt numb, exhausted, but with just an irrepressible glimmer of hope in the pit of my heart and stomach. Maybe—just maybe—this one would surprise us.

His mother was Tatiana, she had good handwriting (why would they mention this?—what did her education or penmanship matter if the child was permanently unwell?), she was twenty years younger than me, and at two and a half months Fyodor was holding his head up, at his current five months he was rolling back and forth on his belly. But he can't sit on his own, they added quickly.

I felt trapped again.

Fyodor was a huge and immobile little dude, with an enormous round head and face and piercing blue eyes. But his body was as stiff as a two-by-four—I was thinking it looked like he might have cerebral palsy or something very dire—and you could tell that he was mad as hell about it, though he was super-cute and looked like my brother had as a baby

I fell in love with Fyodor. His fat cheeks, his obvious determination. After the obligatory, "Isn't he beautiful Russian baby, you so lucky, tomorrow you go to court and sign papers, yes?" while we watched him not move for an hour, we were taken back to the hotel.

I told David that I thought little Fyodor had some kind of paralysis, but my heart went out to him. "If he even has a fighting chance, let's do it." David didn't say anything but did not protest.

But in my heart I knew Fyodor was not at all well.

I went to the hotel office center, paid by the minute to type everything up and fax it—still the only reliable way to send information from Siberia—to New York to await Dr. Aronson's assessment the next morning.

That night we went to the hotel restaurant with some of the other couples, all of whom were joyfully sharing pictures of their smiling, healthy tots and preparing to fly back to their respective homes in the U.S. the next morning.

But we were still in limbo, and I knew little Fyodor didn't look great health-wise. Still, the food in the small restaurant was wonderful—blinis, lots of fish, beets, vodka, and all very inexpensive, so I decided to enjoy the evening and see what tomorrow would bring.

Very High Risk

THE NEXT MORNING, 11:15 A.M., we awaited the call during which Dr. Aronson would give us her opinion as to the health of the baby. Fat little Fyodor...

"Hello?" I said anxiously, my heart once again pounding with nerves and anticipation—how could that crazy organ still feel anything? How many times had I been in this exact position, waiting for news on something over which I had no control, and hoping against hope that with this one, this time, my luck was going to turn?

I checked my watch—11:16 A.M.—maybe this would be the auspicious moment.

"Hi, Dr. Aronson here. Very high risk." She didn't mince words and went on to say that Fyodor's prematurity, his low weight, and the blood transfusion (risk of AIDS, etc.) made it extremely unlikely that he would ever be healthy, so it was a no-go.

It was very, very upsetting.

"He will likely have a lifetime of extreme medical needs, perhaps also mental needs," the doctor said.

I hung up, deflated, like our agency had drop-kicked us yet again. They sent us to freaking Siberia without having an appropriate child for us (probably Scary Natasha had lied to them like she did to us every time she opened her black-lipsticked mouth), and the agency was now flailing around trying to toss any sick kid our way, any one they could pawn off on us. How clueless did they think we were?

I knew that the Natashas would show up soon to cart us off to the office where they expected us to make Fyodor officially ours, and I dreaded yet another lobby stand-off. And sure enough, we got another lecture, Scary Natasha, dark and scowling, wearing head-to-toe black leather, including a skirt a size too small for her ample hips, a skintight black leather jacket, her long jet-black hair framing her puffy, middle-aged, heavily pockmarked and pancaked face. I imagined her cracking a whip and again heard the comical "Frau Blücher" from *Young Frankenstein.* The smiling Nice Natasha kept translating all the while, "You Americans think you're going to get a perfect American baby," then pausing to listen to the scowling Scary Natasha spit something out in Russian, then continuing with a smile, "You must realize that this baby will grow out of this," blah, blah, blah.

I stood immobile, then tried to gently break in. "No, we're not like that, we don't expect perfection, just a child with a fighting chance. We're not rich Americans, we've been trying for a long time to become parents," and so on, but black leather-clad Scary Natasha never let up.

"There are no more children to see, no more orphanages," Nice Natasha translated. Then they turned and left us still standing in the lobby. I remember feeling the emptiness of my arms hanging by my sides rather than cradling the baby we had been promised we would meet.

David and I stood there uncertainly for a few minutes, and when we slowly trudged back up to our room David finally spoke up. "We should just leave…"

"What?" I said. "No way!"

"They're not going to give us a healthy kid, we should get the hell out of here."

I knew how uncomfortable David was with any type of conflict, much less being in Siberia with hostile folks who had confiscated our passports and considered us piggy, spoiled, rich Americans. (Oh, another welcoming fact: then-President George W. Bush had just invaded Afghanistan. "What do you think of this Bush?" they asked us. "Oh, we hate him, we marched against him—we protested!" Scary Natasha and driver Kristofferson still looked like they'd like to see us roasting over a spit.)

"No way," I exclaimed to David. "I am not leaving this continent without my child—we've done 'regular' pregnancy, IVF, domestic adoption, also known as hell—what are we gonna do now? What's left? A Chia Pet baby? I am *not leaving without my baby!*" I had comical visions of some Russian soldiers trying to peel my hands from around a tree and hoist me onto a plane that said, OUTTA HERE while I screamed in protest.

That night we wandered down to the lobby—all the other American couples who hadn't already flown home were again emailing happy photos of their kids to friends and family—and I happened to say hello to the young office area attendant, whose English was pretty good.

"You sending pictures too?" she smiled.

"Me, no, um…we haven't met our child yet."

"Oh?" she said, surprised.

"No, and we've been to both orphanages—we met only very sick children, unfortunately…" My voice trailed off, the exhaustion, disappointment, depression, and tears welling up.

"What mean you, both orphanages. You mean all?" she asked.

"Well, number one and number two," I said quietly.

"Not the rest?" she asked innocently.

I caught my breath. "How many are there?" I asked.

"Oh, well at least nine…" She saw my surprised expression. "My mother is a professor and translator, she has been to many of them."

The image of Scary Natasha rose in my mind, her bulging black leather outfits, her hissing in my face, "There are *no* more orphanages, *no* more babies." Probably no more that were giving her a kickback was more like it.

I gazed out at the gray and soot-streaked hotel window; we were surrounded by other gray, half-finished cinder-block buildings and piles of crusty, black-stained snow.

We were unwelcome strangers in a strange land, and our hosts were clearly corrupt and beyond reason. Nine orphanages, huh? No freaking way—I had come way too far, emotionally, physically, financially, and now geographically—no way in hell I was backing down or leaving empty-handed, Scary Natasha be damned.

Stuck in Siberia

I MUST DIGRESS for a moment. I do not mean in any way to imply that the adoption crisis in Russia, the heartbreak of overflowing and underfunded orphanages, is the fault of the Birth Mothers, who must too often make what has to be a wrenching decision. Or that Russians themselves are anything other than a very proud, beautiful, deep, and cultured people. (I feel very in touch with my own Russian ancestry and went there feeling as though I were returning to my homeland.)

The Russian adoption quagmire has been utterly stalled since December 2012, when Vladimir Putin enacted the Dima Yakovlev Law, Russian federal law number 272-FZ, banning the adoption of Russian children by U.S. citizens. (Putin did it in retaliation for Obama having enacted a common sense law around Russian billionaires and where they put their wealth.)

Adoption in Russia has apparently long been a lucrative business for otherwise often extremely poor Russian citizens and officials, but the obvious issues with their system seem to stem rather from a whole series of deeply entrenched and complex issues: the lack of choice for women in terms of family planning; the lack of employment and opportunity for women and families to feel capable of providing for children; cultural pride and shame, all tied in to what seems to be an overall culture that celebrates machismo and male strength; the huge disparities, now so sadly prevalent the world over, between the haves and the have-nots. Not to mention alcoholism. My own mother was herself deposited in an orphanage for a few years by her Russian immigrant mother in mid-century, mid-Depression Chicago while her mother attended beauty school, working to secure a way to provide for her two children as a then-rare single mother. I get it—we women do what we have to do—always have, always will, even if it means making impossible decisions to take care of one's own family.

All the more the shame then that our worldly, largely educated countries have not yet been able to figure out how to better support women—and to hold men more accountable for their contributions—which inevitably directly affects children and their security. That and the fact that everything—even children—now seems to have entered the realm of business opportunity, a feeling that was sadly prevalent during the entire international adoption process and especially during my time in Russia.

And so…

By the next morning, all the other couples had flown home via Moscow back to the U.S., full of joy and cute photos and thrilled that they had met the children they would soon return to pick up and take to their permanent homes.

The Natashas appeared once again and we were silently driven back to Orphanage Number 2 where we were to meet a six-month-old girl. During the tense drive, I mentioned that we had been told that there were at least nine orphanages in the town.

Nice Natasha relayed this to Scary Natasha, who did not even bother to look my way in the backseat but simply spat out a few monosyllabic-sounding words, *"Nyet"* being the only one I clearly understood.

Nice Natasha smiled in my direction. "She say no, only the two that we work with. Nothing else."

I was about to disagree and insist that we be taken to some other place, a different orphanage, but decided better of it—the best option at this point was simply to placate them today and head back to Moscow or somewhere else as soon as we possibly could. Of course, unless a miracle happened and this next girl we were to meet was half-way healthy, but I knew the odds of that happening were microscopic.

Back in stale-smelling, depressing Orphanage Number 2, after we had given the officials their gifts of coffee and candies as instructed, not to mention the hundreds of dollars in cash we forked over every time we stepped into one of the orphanages (it had been made clear to us that only brand-new, crisp American dollars were acceptable, and nothing under a twenty-dollar bill), we met a little girl named Svetlana who was about six months old. Again, we went through the motions, the resident doctor rattling off statistics and me dutifully scribbling them down to relay to Dr. Aronson. When they said they had no head circumference measurement an alarm sounded in my head. Did they think we had forgotten the very sick kids we had met previously?

"Svetlana has rickets, a vitamin D/sun deficiency but is no big deal," Nice Natasha translated, "and she can't open her legs wide, as her hips are weak."

I had a sinking feeling.

"Are you sure you don't have her head circumference?" I asked, my voice small with exhaustion despite my renewed determination.

The doctor dug around for a minute and then spoke, Nice Natasha translating. "Her head circumference is now thirty-six point five." I knew that her head circumference at that age should be at least thirty-nine or forty. Even Fyodor's was thirty-eight point four, and Dr. Aronson had been worried about that!

After the cursory "play time" with little Svetlana, who was almost as stiff as had been Fyodor and not much more robust looking than the poor little other baby girl we had met, I left feeling absolutely dejected, depressed, and worried that perhaps the Kristofferson look-alike driver and Scary Natasha would simply drive us into the Siberian wilderness and shove us out of the car.

I thought back on the last seventy-two hours, which seemed like a lifetime. A hellish lifetime. So many sad, sickly, abandoned children, many with little or no prospect of every finding a permanent home or a healthy life. So many *babushkas* doing the best they could with way too little of everything—too little food, too little clothing, too little time and attention.

"I don't think you should talk to that doctor of yours anymore," Nice Natasha relayed from Scary Natasha. "Our Russian doctors are here, they see these beautiful Russian babies, they know, they positive, that these babies all grow up strong and healthy."

They resented us, considered us ugly, probably rich, spoiled Americans. Which in comparison, I suppose we were.

Despite their apparent resentment of us, everyone in Siberia held out a hand to be greased and was more than happy to take our American dollars. There was not even an attempt to hide the blatant corruption and bribery. We had been warned that we would be expected to bring "gifts" everywhere we went, but actually experiencing the expectation of payment during an attempted adoption still felt shocking, especially since there were clearly thousands of children desperate for permanent homes. One of the local agency reps in Moscow had commented on it as she warned us not to be intimidated by any of the locals' bluster. "Why don't they adopt these children themselves if they resent Americans doing it so much?"

The next morning, after Dr. Aronson had read over the details I had sent her about Svetlana, when the phone rang she didn't even say hi.

"Why can't they get you a healthy baby? This baby—Svetlana—her head circumference is abysmal." Despite how heartbreaking the facts were, hearing Dr. Aronson be so solidly on our side in finding a healthy baby was overwhelming and I had to fight back tears.

Dr. Aronson continued, clearly irritated. "Do you mind if I call the head of your adoption agency?"

"They threatened to throw us out of the country, to send us back to Moscow..." I said.

"That's bullshit," Dr. Aronson interrupted. "They can't do anything to you—stick to your guns, don't listen to their threats!" I wanted to cheer! "There are great referrals out there," she added, "I have said, 'This one looks great!' to plenty of adoptive parents. Don't accept anything that doesn't thrill you."

I hung up the phone feeling more hopeful—I was gonna get *out* of Siberia one way or the other, back to civilization where we might have a team that actually wanted to help us and not just fleece us for our American cash and stick us with a seriously ill child.

And that night, in what felt like a sign from God, I turned on the ancient TV in the room and discovered that "Sex and the City" was on, and it was great even in Russian!

Later that night I called Wendy, our U.S. agency rep, and told her how horribly everything had been going. "If the next referral doesn't work out, do *not* come home," she said.

"We couldn't leave if we wanted to," I reminded her, "they confiscated our passports.

"We don't want another referral here," I told her. "They are not on our side, everyone is corrupt, especially your local rep Natasha, and they will never show us any healthy kids—we *have* to get out of here!"

Wendy said nothing so I continued. "Send us to a neighboring town, back to Moscow, anywhere—we'll drive, fly, take a dog sled—anything!"

Wendy said that she had to speak with Yuri before we could make other plans. (Yuri was then the head of the agency's Russian adoption program but was later convicted of fraud and some type of bribery and I think even ended up in jail.) Local rep Scary Natasha was supposedly reporting back to him so he knew what was happening—who knew what she was telling him, probably a pack of lies—but we still couldn't reach him or make any further plans.

I slept a few fitful hours and awoke exhausted but hoping to hear news that we were being sent to a different region. I noted to myself that we had been scheduled to fly home out of Moscow the following day, but that did not look likely at this point.

Finally, we heard from the U.S. adoption agency that we were heading back to Moscow the next morning. "You will fly back to Moscow tomorrow morning at 7 A.M., be picked up at the airport by the head of the Moscow office, and go to meet a referral [child]."

"Um, great, wow, okay…"

"Better call the airline, the fees are steep to make changes."

"Okay, will do, thanks. Should we…?"

The phone went dead. *Alrighty then,* I thought. *At least we're getting out of here in one piece.*

The phone rang again and I assumed it was the U.S. agency again.

"Yes?" I answered.

"Be downstairs in twenty minutes and bring all your documents."

"Natasha?" I asked.

"*Dah.* Downstairs." She hung up.

Achtung, I muttered to myself. The whole thing felt so shady, so clandestine, like something out of an old spy novel. I reminded myself that we were here on this giant continent trying to do something positive, to give a fighting chance to a child who, judging from what we had seen thus far, might otherwise have a very short and joyless life.

We gathered the large accordion folder that held all of our papers and waited dutifully downstairs, not knowing where we might be going. Or when. I felt completely at the mercy of our agency and the least kind person on our Siberian "team," Scary Natasha, not a comforting feeling. If we could just get through the next twenty-four hours, we would be heading back to Moscow and hopefully to the company of representatives who wanted to work with us and not against us.

As I sat in the dreary Siberian lobby, with an exit flight within sight, I felt utterly drained, having been hustled into and out of two very depressing orphanages, seeing nothing but fatally unwell children whose lives were likely to be short and painful. Not to mention the arduous road that had led us to Russia in the first place.

The Natashas appeared and told us that we had to go to the regional notary to officially decline our "referrals," the name for the children we had been shown as possible adoptees. "You explain why you no accept any of the beautiful Russian babies we show you," Nice Natasha interpreted, her warm smile the usual bizarre contrast to the hissing scowl of Scary Natasha.

We were driven to a large, austere yet imposing brick-and-cement building with marble columns everywhere. Once inside, our footsteps echoed throughout the wide, bare hallways, the overall feeling being one of a grandeur gone stale.

We were ushered into an even mustier-smelling office where an old man pulled out a gigantic, heavy, leather-bound book that looked like its pages were made of ancient parchment. He carefully set it down on the counter and beckoned for us to sign our names. Scary Natasha continued to glare throughout. The whole tableau was very theatrical, practically campy, including Scary Natasha's constant rudeness, which was starting to seem almost comical now that I knew we were leaving at dawn on the next flight out.

That night I felt exhausted by the whole Siberian ordeal and fell into what felt like a heavy sleep. The phone rang and I leapt out of bed, thinking it was our four A.M. wakeup call to get to the airport. I picked it up and it was Wendy from our U.S. agency. (It was eleven P.M., I'd only been asleep for about fifteen minutes but was so exhausted that I thought it was morning.)

Wendy assured me that she'd spoken with Yuri, and that we would be taken care of in Moscow, that we would be given more than one referral if necessary, that we would go to see an American doctor and that, God forbid, if none of the Moscow kids was healthy, we would not be drummed out of town as nasty Scary Natasha had threatened.

I went back to sleep, looking forward to boarding a plane out of there the next day, and allowing myself just the faintest glimmer of hope that there might be a healthy baby waiting for us in Moscow.

No, No Novokuznetsk

WE WERE FINALLY heading out of Siberia which was thrilling, but it was painful economically as well as emotionally; the hotel ended up costing an extra $300 (an exorbitant amount in Russian terms when the ordinary salary at the time was roughly equivalent to $20 American a month), and changing our airline fares cost an extra $1,100, an enormous sum I imagined they could never get away with charging to a Russian. It was an obvious rip-off, blatant price gouging, but they knew they had us since there was virtually no other choice if we wanted to be given back our passports and leave the area.

Saturday, March 22, 7 A.M.
We were leaving Siberia—finally!—and heading back to Moscow. I felt like I could exhale and in some small way let go of some of the heartbreak of the last few days, which had felt like an emotional lifetime. But with that sense of relief came a wave of the many emotions and feelings that I had been holding at arm's length every second of every day to be able to keep putting one foot in front of the other and make it through each gut-wrenching experience.

I had had no choice but to keep on waking up every day and going through with whatever plan our local captors had in store for us, but the whole thing had left me with an overwhelming sense of sadness, and virtually everything seemed bleak, hopeless. What would become of all those poor, unwell babies? I couldn't let myself follow that thought, it was too horrifying. I felt as though I were living in a worst-case scenario nightmare from which I could not awake, as depressing as the soot-stained mounds of snow outside our hotel window.

But even smashed into the tiny backseat of the tiny car, I couldn't help but marvel at the timelessness of the landscape, the sense of futility it inspired—there was no visual relief in sight, no beauty, no greenery, just snow and soot and more snow. I thought, no wonder there are so many deeply angst-ridden, philosophical writers from Russia—there's nothing else here except space, cold, grime, and your thoughts.

Still, it had been a surprisingly satisfying feeling, wrenching my passport out of the hands of the scowling desk clerk back in the hotel, and even when we got to the airport and climbed the stairs back onto the duct-taped airplane, I had an overwhelming sense of having escaped a possibly dangerous fate; whether it be the unspoken threat of one of our "hosts" or being subjected to their constant coercion that we adopt an obviously very sick child, I reminded myself that we were good people, that we were simply trying to expand our family and ideally to do something good on this planet, not do anything dastardly or harmful.

Outside the airplane window, Siberia stretched endlessly below me. I dozed off and woke forty minutes later. Still nothing but wheat-colored, snow-covered plains as far as the eye could see, with an occasional pop of green or a cluster of ramshackle houses.

I leaned my head back and closed my eyes and couldn't help but smile just a little.

Amazingly, nonsensically, I started to think of the Siberian adventure as almost comically bad, notwithstanding of course the tragedy of those many, many sick children. But I had to keep moving forward, and a glimmer of my sense of humor was in view; that and hope, that fiendishly reoccurring friend, were edging back into my heart.

I had truly come to understand the phrase "Hope springs eternal." Just when your life, the entire world, looked bleak and unending, one tiny word of optimism and encouragement could bring hope surging back. You could run hope over with a steamroller, and back up it would pop. Hit it with a sledgehammer, and still it returned. Drop it from a plane, throw it from the roof, it just kept bouncing back, despite logic, the odds, or common sense.

So there we were, en route back to Moscow, having agreed to try to have fun, to enjoy the city, and to look forward to hopefully (that word again!) meeting Pinky, our soon-to-be child.

I felt terrible and heartsick about the seriously ill children we had met, including the stony-faced, blank-eyed girls and Fyodor, the fat-cheeked, immobile baby boy I had fallen in love with. I wished them health and forever families or at least some comfort and love during what might be short lives.

Moscow

Saturday, March 22, afternoon

IN MOSCOW, WE WERE MET at the airport by our adoption agency's Moscow office chief, a no-nonsense but friendly middle-aged woman, as well as an interpreter and a driver, and then were taken to the Moscow office and made to sign another parchment book promising that we would be honest, and that our intentions were good, and that we wouldn't turn down any "healthy, beautiful Russian babies" (that again).

Then we were shown a tiny little picture, maybe only a square inch in size, of a goofy-looking newborn baby boy (goofy in the way that all newborns look goofy, like doughy, cross-eyed aliens).

They started to explain. "This is Ivan [his given name—I wonder why Russians give kids names even when they are putting them up for adoption?] and he is seven months old." My heart sank—why were they showing us a photo of a newborn if this boy was now seven months old? What's wrong with *this* poor kid?

"You know, Russian families adopt all the baby girls, especially if have blue eyes," the agency head reminded us with a smile, as though it were common knowledge. "So no girls, just boys now."

I kept listening.

We were told that this baby boy had been born prematurely and weighed what I calculated to be only a few pounds at birth, and then had pneumonia for the first six months of his life so had remained hospitalized, and then had been taken to the orphanage. He at that point weighed about eleven pounds, the norm being closer to eighteen pounds for a baby boy his age. Apparently, he had stayed in the orphanage briefly, gotten very sick again, been taken back to the hospital a few times, and was now back at the orphanage.

This did not bode well.

"Let's go." The agency head, kindly though clearly the Boss, stood to leave.

What—now? I thought. We had just barely slept, flown for over five hours, then gotten shuttled from the airport directly here. Now we're to drive an hour or two outside Moscow to another orphanage to meet this boy?

But what alternative was there?

"Okay," I said, stood and followed her out the door.

*The Orphanage
(or, 90 Minutes and
100 Years Outside of Moscow)*

WE DROVE ABOUT FIFTY-FIVE MILES and what felt like 100 years back in time from Moscow; as soon as we maneuvered past the famously congested roundabouts in downtown Moscow, with snarled traffic honking and zigzagging everywhere, flying towards and veering away from us on all sides at seeming random, we headed southeast towards the town of Ramenskoye (famous for an aeronautics industry, among other things), where tiny little Ivan was apparently recently again out of the hospital and back in the orphanage.

We left the bustling city streets, famous for gridlocked highways, and gradually found ourselves in the countryside; with every mile we got farther outside of Moscow, we seemed to go back another era in time. First, we passed cinderblock apartment houses, mostly large and square and bleakly nondescript, with bits of frozen snow outlining them and fewer and fewer cars passing us on the road. Another few miles and the fields got broader and the apartment blocks turned to small wooden houses, with one that looked right out of an old fairy tale; it was probably twenty feet square with a beautiful carved wooden outline of crescent moons and other small shapes all along its roofline. There was what I presumed to be a small outhouse a few feet away. All the fields around it were frozen brown and gray, and I couldn't help but imagine how long that tiny house had stood there, what history it had seen march past it, what children and grandparents might have run around rich fields in springtime or chipped away chunks of ice in winter.

"That's the governor's mansion," our interpreter said as we passed a gated driveway, a huge house visible behind a snowdrift.

I was nervous and excited—would this be our child?—but was utterly wrung out from all our travails and I couldn't muster as much emotion as I had previously, wondering whether this would be the Moment.

I started to comment out loud on the disparity in the different communities—some looked like century-old shacks untouched by hammer or nail since they were erected, while others were clearly homes for the elite with electric security fences, posh, cypress-lined driveways, and windowed second stories. But then I realized that everyone in the tiny 1970-style Toyota Corolla car was asleep except for me and the driver; in the backseat were crammed David, the translator, and I; in the front seat were the driver and the head of the Moscow agency.

I caught the driver's eye in the rearview mirror and he nodded silently, and I turned my attention back to the landscape around us.

The roads went from well paved near Moscow to more rutted as the city turned to countryside, the snow-packed roads sometimes plowed and sometimes not.

We pulled off the highway and onto a heavily rutted dirt road, the car bouncing so violently on the rocky dirt road that everybody woke up. We passed country houses and industrial, generic-looking buildings, and steered around a man drunkenly weaving his way down the road with a pack of skinny, mangy dogs trailing him. I wouldn't want to be out there after dark, I thought.

We turned a corner and crossed some railroad tracks (literally, the other side of the tracks), and pulled to a stop in front of a modest, two-story brown building.

"Here we are," our leader said.

Now I was getting nervous.

Ivan of Ramenskoye (or, He's Alive)

RAMENSKOYE, RUSSIA, WAS apparently first mentioned in historical terms around 1328 and now has a population of roughly 100,000 people. Known for its aeronautics industry, particularly a flight research institute, history says that a stone church was built there in about 1725.

As I went through a small gate, across a neat yard, and up a few stairs towards the orphanage's doublewide front door, my numbness began to thaw; it had been such a long, long journey to be right here. What would be on the other side of the door? Would it be another disappointment, a child with no chance to live a full or healthy life?

The large front door was opened and inside the air was warm but did not have the putrid, dank smell of the other orphanages we had seen in Siberia. Into the small doctor's office we went for the briefing.

Ivan, aka Vanya (I thought of *Uncle Vanya*, of course), was born on August 9, 2002 in the town of Lubertz and had arrived in the orphanage around September 12, but had been back to the hospital and then returned back to the orphanage around November 1.

They told us about his parents—supposedly a married couple, unusual for an adoption scenario, though at that point I took everything with a grain of salt in terms of actual facts—who already had two kids and couldn't afford another. He had been a hidden pregnancy—it is not uncommon for women in Russia to hide pregnancies when they are going to put the kids up for adoption, or conversely, to pretend to be pregnant when they are not and are in fact adopting a child—so presumably there had been zero prenatal care. He had been born about two months premature and weighed roughly two pounds at birth and had been in the neonatal intensive care unit for six months. Poor little guy, I thought—no one there to sing to him, hold and rock him, to fight for him.

They said that he had jaundice, pneumonia, prenatal encephalopathy (a catchall phrase they used for overall lousy health), a cold, an ear infection, was anemic, and had rickets.

Wow.

Now, however, they said he smiled, tried to stand, had "good eyes" (meaning he made eye contact, I supposed), recognized his caretakers, could roll over and hold toys. He could not sit up yet, they told us. They told us about his diet—soup, minced meat, dairy, egg yolk, mashed veggies, cereal, juices—and that his muscle tone was "tense" but that he was strong.

"OK, you meet him." We all stood and David and I followed the crew to a bright and airy sunroom the size and look of a small ballet studio with mirrors across one entire wall and another wall of picture windows looking out on a play area. There were blue-and-white floral designs painted onto the white walls and overall the place was a lot cheerier than anything we had thus far seen.

We stood uneasily in the room waiting for Vanya. We paced, joking nervously. I guess the interpreter and agency rep sat in there too but I can't recall.

I felt like an electrical hum was coursing through me, waiting to see what state little Vanya would be in, too wounded to fantasize that this would indeed be my Pinky.

Finally, the door opened. A smiling *babushka* stepped in, wearing a traditional-looking headscarf and smock, and cradling a tiny little bundle of baby, tightly swaddled in a mismatch of patched blankets. The baby's face just barely peeked out of the blankets, his eyes wide, darting back and forth around the room, taking everything in. He looked extremely alert, scared, but definitely *in there*, aware, a stunning contrast to the barely alive babies we had met in Siberia.

Without thinking, I said to myself, "He's alive."

The *babushka* walked over and handed me the baby. I held him, looked down at his tiny face, his terrified expression, his amber colored eyes. "Hi Vanya," I smiled.

Could He Be the One?

AFTER THE SURREAL AND exhausting week in Siberia, the flight back to Moscow, and getting hustled from the airport to the adoption office to an embassy, then driving straight out to yet one more orphanage, I was too drained to be very excited, too wrung out for that fluttery feeling of "I'm about to meet my baby!"

Still, tiny little Vanya, with his handsome face, his determined "is that all you got, world?" expression, was clearly the most alive and vibrant of all the babies we had met. We did the obligatory Russian baby meet-and-greet though Vanya was clearly unwell—his eyelids were droopy, his expression looked like he felt seasick, he was limp in some body parts and stiff as a board in others, and even this much activity exhausted him.

As we were driven back towards Moscow an hour later, I thought of all that had just happened. I had held Vanya, moved a finger left and right for his eyes to follow (they did), made noises to see if he could hear well enough to turn his head to see what made them (he could), touched all his fingers and toes to make sure he was responsive (he was), and generally tried to get a sense of his health and awareness. The *babushkas* were right—he did have "good eyes," meaning he seemed comfortable making eye contact and was alert and focused.

Although he was tiny and looked more like a three-month-old than a seven-month-old, and although he was stiff and had clearly never moved much physically, little Vanya began to feel like a potentially healthy prospect and the gray haze over my exhausted heart began to clear. I closed my eyes to recall his perfect little face, his perfect tiny nose, his little cleft chin, his eyes a mix of green and brown (apparently just like my mother's Russian mother).

After we held and played with Vanya, he was clearly exhausted, and they came and took him away back through the big doors to wherever he lived. Even though I was drained of emotion, I felt for this tiny little baby boy who was clearly a fighter and desperate for all kinds of attention, and it seemed odd in comparison to leave him in his orphanage and check ourselves into Moscow's Marriott Hotel, which seemed the very pinnacle of luxury after our week in Siberia.

When I called Dr. Aronson later, she suggested not only that we take a video of Vanya for her to see—seeing as how we were all skeptical about getting a healthy referral after the debacle in Siberia—but also that we hire a former medical student of hers (Dr. Aronson taught pediatric medicine at her alma mater Cornell University), now a pediatrician herself who happened to be temporarily living in Moscow with her husband.

I agreed and checked my video "to do" list: make sure to get him pulling to a stand, cruising along the crib, transferring items hand to hand. At seven months, I was told, there is usually a four-month delay responding to sound and touch for the average orphanage baby. And I was also to use the list to check off the child's activities. Dr. Aronson reminded me to summarize simply, "He sat down on his own, made a vowel sound, etc." I was also to include my impressions, like did he make eye contact or connect with his caregiver or other kids?

I was to take and send digital photos to Dr. Aronson, including a closeup of Vanya's face, his profile, and any birthmarks or deformities.

I called Dr. Aronson's protégé, Dr. Melissa, who was about my age, and she agreed to come the next morning to examine Vanya. The orphanage was a bit prickly at first when our interpreter asked their permission to have an outside doctor examine him—everything had to be done strictly by the book, any little surprise could upset the whole process—but they eventually agreed.

We picked up Dr. Melissa the next morning and drove once again out to the orphanage, where I watched and aided as Dr. Melissa stripped Vanya naked and gently poked and prodded him for a good hour, giving him a thorough baby exam.

Looking at this tiny little baby, naked on the plastic-covered mattress/couch in the large room with the blue designs on the wall, he seemed so helpless; his stomach was hugely distended like pictures of third-world refugees I had seen, his legs limp and useless, his arms seemingly permanently bent at the elbow. Yet there was a fierceness to him, the same glimmer I had seen when we first met that had made me mutter, "He's alive."

When Dr. Melissa held him in a certain position to see if he could manage a specific physical task, like reach across his body with one arm, his lack of strength made it look impossible but somehow he would muster the muscle to do it. He reached for a rattle, he rolled from one side to the other, he even tried to crawl by pulling himself along on his tiny bent elbows.

"I don't think he's ever had the chance to move at all," Dr. Melissa said. "My guess is that he lives in a crib with a few other babies." I looked at her with alarm. "It's not uncommon," she continued. "They don't have enough of anything, food, clothing, care, to go around so those children that are the strongest get taken care of first. Survival of the fittest if you will."

"Wow…" I stammered, imagining poor little Vanya trying to get the basics he needed to survive.

"This orphanage is nicer than most I've seen," Dr. Melissa added. And it was true—the place was clean and bright, and the women who worked there—and in the many orphanages we had seen, there had not been one single man in sight, solely women—seemed as kind and attentive as they could be under the circumstances.

Vanya was a sport throughout the exam, never crying or getting impatient, but was clearly exhausted near the end. Eventually he got so tired that he could barely hold his head up.

By this time, I was falling in love with Vanya and silently rooting for him to get even a moderately healthy prognosis. Dr. Melissa remained sweet and kind but didn't reveal much as we made the drive back to Moscow, where she was to email and then discuss her report with Dr. Aronson, who would then give us a call at four o'clock that afternoon with her estimate of Vanya's health and whether she considered him a low, moderate, or high risk.

We got back to the hotel around noon. After all the ins and outs and ups and downs of the past week, there was no way I could spend four long hours sitting around the hotel room waiting for Dr. Aronson's phone call and verdict, so we decided to head out into the freezing wet Moscow afternoon to a local theater museum. I felt a sense of pride at my Russian roots as I looked at the gorgeous and serious displays of theater scenes, sketches, and costumes, all from past productions of Russian classics.

Afterwards, with still a few hours until the witching hour of four o'clock and our Dr. Aronson phone call, we had lunch and then walked past statues and shops, constantly watching the clock as the minutes ticked off.

After all the years it had taken to get to this exact moment, it now felt like time was standing still. My emotions were scrubbed raw, the highs and lows and wishes and dreams, the disappointments and new goals and affirmations of the last few years that felt like eons—all of it had worn me down to a dull nub.

But now here I was, on a street in Moscow, a gentle snow dappling the sidewalk, the colorful turrets of the amazing architecture everywhere I looked—could I dare allow myself to think that little Vanya was the one, that he was the Pinky for whom I had been so long searching? Maybe he had been waiting for someone just like us, like me, to come and find him? Would he get the okay, a thumbs-up, or at least a half-promising sideways, from Doctors Aronson and Melissa?

I couldn't think of anything else yet didn't dare let myself imagine an actual outcome. It was as though my heart were as frozen as the landscape around me, a beautiful contradiction, at once both dazzling with color and shape yet desolate and forbidding, both delicate and unbreakable. I remember feeling the blood pulse through my body as I stood there in the snow and I felt incredibly, vibrantly alive, numb, eternal, as though I were frozen in the exact spot on the planet I was meant to occupy in that precise moment.

Pins and Needles

I WAS GETTING MORE and more nervous as each minute passed—
would Dr. Aronson say low risk? I could even live with moderate risk.
I couldn't bear the thought of little Vanya being left to languish in
the orphanage, where they were kind but obviously lacked adequate
food, clothing, medicine, and staff.

After what seemed like a year's worth of minutes, it was 3:30.
Time to head slowly back towards the hotel to await Dr. Aronson's
call. I stopped and looked in a few shop windows. 3:40. I didn't want
to get there a minute too soon since I felt like the nervous anticipation would kill me.

We walked another few blocks. 3:50. Time to go! We sprinted
though the snow the final block back to the Marriott, crossed the
lobby quickly, and hit the elevator button.

My heart was pounding in my ears. In a few minutes I would find
out whether it was likely, or rather advisable from a health perspective, that this beautiful little baby, this neglected and determined
child, would become my son.

I opened the hotel door quickly, dropped my winter coat on the
bed and shook the cold out of my hair. I reminded myself to breathe.
It was exactly 4:00.

A minute passed. Then another. In my mind I thought that
maybe Dr. Aronson was trying to find the right words to tell us that
yet another baby was high risk. I swept the idea from my mind.
Besides, Vanya's eyes had been so defiantly alive!

The phone rang. My heart stopped. I picked it up.

"Hello?"

"Congratulations…" Dr. Aronson said.

She continued on but I couldn't hear anything she was saying because I was sobbing, screaming, jumping up and down in a circle, two feet off the floor.

It was unbelievable! I was elated, also a little scared—he was so tiny and sickly!—but I had seen his face! I had looked into his eyes! I knew he was in there! Finally, irretrievably, my Pinky!

I couldn't wait to hold and comfort him, to ease the worries so evident even on his tiny baby face, to promise him I would take care of him forever.

I realized afterwards that we had met Ivan, aka Vanya, aka Pinky, aka Stephan, on March 21, the first day of spring. After all those years of attributing significance to the least little thing, of wishing and hoping that each holiday date would somehow become the Day, finally we had a momentous date with a momentous occasion to match!

When I regained a bit of composure, I got back on the phone with Dr. Aronson.

"You know," she said, "I was prepared to get a bad report from Dr. Melissa and thought that we'd have to decline yet another referral, but I'm surprised and happy to say that he looks OK, all things considered! Plenty of challenges ahead, but OK and with a tenacious spirit!"

She wished us a safe flight home and congratulated us again.

We rushed down to the hotel lobby—I had found out that their landline cost one-tenth the amount our cellphones or the room phone did—and called my mom.

"It's a boy!" I sobbed into the phone. Russians around the lobby glared at me, obviously still resentful that Americans were coming to "take" their "beautiful Russian babies." *Tough shit*, I thought—*this one's mine!*

The next day we went back to the orphanage to spend more time with Vanya. He looked awful, pale and droopy-eyed, drained, like he felt terrible both physically and mentally. The exam from the previous day was perhaps more physical activity than he had ever done in his life and had worn him completely out.

I held him gently against my chest and he fell deeply asleep, his tiny head on my shoulder. I wished I could take him home right then and there—why on earth did we have to wait for three more months and come back for a second trip to bring him home? It was of course all about money, Russian adoption at least at that point being a business first and foremost—but I couldn't bear the thought of my sweet, sickly, tiny baby boy missing out on food or care or the love he deserved and so desperately needed.

I held and rocked Vanya until they came to take him back. He was limp, listless. I hoped he would be able to muster the strength to survive until I could come back and bring him permanently home. I reluctantly handed him over and then I watched as he disappeared, wrapped in the *babushka's* arms, behind the blue-and-white wooden doors. I stood there, almost afraid to breathe lest I break out in tears or wake up from this dream, until the heavy doors slowly slammed shut behind him.

The Waiting (Trip Number 2)

THE FLIGHT BACK TO New York seemed endless, my mind constantly seeing the little face of Vanya, aka Ivan, now officially named Stephan, as he had disappeared behind the big blue-and-white wooden doors, his expression so sweet, so exhausted, so needy. It was going to be a long wait until I could go back, scoop him up, and bring him permanently home.

I dove back in to work and expected I would hear from our agency "any time" about our return trip. Some of the people we had traveled with had gotten their court dates to pick up their kids within two weeks! "It won't take longer than three or four weeks to get your court date," they said. Getting a court date meant you would fly back to Russia just prior to that date and be ready to go before a judge and—hopefully—officially become a child's adoptive parent.

A month went by. Then Mother's Day rolled around again. Sigh.

"Oh, we heard that now it could be up to six weeks before you get a court date," our agency said. I cringed. "And they need more documents…"

Good God, I thought—I had already sent them virtually every meaningful record of my and David's lives, apart and together, had them notarized and apostilled and copied in triplicate what else could they possibly need? Especially when so many thousands of kids were languishing in under-funded orphanages in every single town all across the gigantic continent, did it really matter if a city notary had signed a two-decade-old document in blue or black ink?

Waiting, waiting, waiting. I worked like crazy, trying to distract myself. David was constantly out of town; I was doing life solo, having definite concerns about the strength of our union and where exactly David was spending all those work hours. Still, my main thought remained of my sweet Stephan, and imagining him in my arms pulled me through the seemingly endless days and nights.

And then, one day at work, my assistant called out. "It's your adoption agency," she said.

I grabbed the phone. Our court date was to be May 20. I checked the date and it was May 13! We had to be in Russia on May 17, in just four days!

I scrambled to make arrangements—book flights, hotels, check passports, Xerox more documents, etc.

I checked my list at home again and again: the dossier (again!), diapers, at least six baby outfits, jammies, bottles and nipples, American baby formula (just in case, although we would get the Russian stuff there that Stephan was used to), a special blankie, stuffed toy, etc.

Finally, the day arrived and we left to return to Russia and bring our little Stephan irrevocably, permanently, *home.*

He's Coming Home!

THE OVERNIGHT AEROFLOT flight from NYC to Moscow was uneventful, and they even had decent food.

Moscow that May was a surprisingly balmy seventy-five degrees, the sun was up from five A.M. until eleven P.M., and the air already had the hint of the mega-humidity that people said made the sweltering summers far worse than the icy winters. It was clear we were in a whole different hemisphere.

We were staying at the Hotel Russia, then the largest single-building hotel in the world with about 10,000 rooms. I almost got lost more than once. The whole place felt and smelled rather seedy, as though not a wall had been painted nor a single sensible putty-colored chair moved since the Soviet-era 1950s. The lobby guard made me show my front desk–issued pass card every time I came or went. (When David said the first day to the guard, "She's my wife," the man just nodded as if to say, "Sure pal, they're all our wives." When we saw what looked like a bunch of call girls in the bar downstairs, I laughed that the guard had imagined I was one of them.)

Our room was on the eighth floor, down a long, Soviet-era hallway that was musty and smelled like an old frat party or dirty underwear. It was dingy at best. The muggy May heat permeated everything and the air was stifling. The upside was the view—we looked out a large window onto Red Square, the amazing, colorful turrets of the tall buildings, the passersby on the street below. I could have sat by the window for days watching the world pass by.

When I again saw Vanya, aka Stephan, I was bowled over by his cuteness! With our interpreter Anna, we took him to get his picture taken for a passport and visa and so had to drive around the suburbs of Ramenskoye near the orphanage. Stephan's eyes were wide the whole time, though he didn't make a peep; he looked like he was trying to absorb the entire world around him. (He'd probably never been in a car before besides going to and from the hospital, and then he was likely restrained.)

Since there were no quickie photo developers to be found (and no easy cellphone pictures back then), we ended up buying a cheapie camera near Red Square and Anna took the photos we snapped—us holding Stephan, Stephan looking at me, Stephan on the floor near us, etc.—to a one-hour photo, and then we piled back into the car and rushed back towards Moscow for our court date.

The court date was where the would-be adoptive parents—in this case, David and I—went before a Russian judge to formally and with finality become the child's adoptive parents. The judge would have the power to grant or deny the adoption request, a chilling thought—especially given the sometimes extreme personalities we had encountered during our Russian adoption adventure—but we were assured that most adoptions were granted and that we were "perfect candidates."

We were told that our judge was tough and were instructed to never look directly at her (what, would we go blind? I thought but did not say), but I had prepared some words to say if I got the chance to speak, to tell her how long we had been trying to become parents, how much love we had for each other and how I felt that Stephan was meant to be my son, how I was meant to be his one and only forever mother. But after the stern young judge, who was dressed in a tank top and peasant skirt as though she were strolling the Venice boardwalk with a guitar, asked some terse questions—address, job title, income, etc.—when the time came and she asked if we had anything to say, I was so choked up with emotion that all I could sputter was, "We think that he was meant to be our son."

The judge left the room and we were left standing there, shushed by our interpreter and feeling like my life literally hung in the balance. Where had the judge gone? Was she getting coffee or looking over some secret file of what kind of people they thought we really were? Was she considering the fact that we had turned down four "beautiful Russian babies" in Siberia?

Finally, the young judge came back into the room. She asked us to stand, which we did though my legs were wobbly with excitement and terror. The judge said, with the hint of a smile, that she was granting the adoption and waiving the ten-day waiting period (another randomly assigned delay presumably done by bureaucrats looking to squeeze more dollars out of the adoption business).

The judge banged her gavel and it jarred me back to the incredible, unbelievable, so long-awaited moment.

Presto, Stephan was our son! I was his mother! I couldn't wait to grab him and smooch his tiny cheeks and never, ever let him go!

We were ushered back out into the hallway where I couldn't hold back my tears, the emotions gushing out of me as though my entire psyche could suddenly exhale. It was not a pretty cry, the release of all the years of waiting and hoping and searching for Pinky making it impossible for me to utter a word but only emit joyous sobbing hiccups.

A few minutes later, after I had regained my composure, we went to the equivalent of City Hall to get our adoption decree and joined a lobby full of waiting people: a young couple draped all over each other (marriage license?), a toothless old woman mumbling to herself. Finally, it was our turn and we signed an official-looking document in a large, tidy office with red chairs and a lovely red patterned rug.

Next, we were taken to the office of the notary, which we had visited on our first trip (and there we saw the same old man who interpreter Anna said always flirted with her). We signed another document in a parchment-looking book and the man shook our hands and wished us well.

That night we had dinner in a hunting lodge–looking place with fancy service and mediocre food. It was very expensive (same as everywhere in Moscow), and we got a little tanked on wine with dinner and grappa afterwards.

The next day we went back to the orphanage where we would pick up Stephan. He would never have to go back there ever again. We were busting him out!

I had packed a beautiful blue baby outfit that my dear friend Nancy had given me, and that was to be Stephan's traveling outfit. He looked so cute and handsome, his tiny little arms still wan and sickly and barely straight enough to make it out of the cuffs. As instructed, we gave boxes of sweets as gifts to the orphanage director and doctor and then piled the tiny blue Stephan into the car to head back to our Moscow hotel and towards the rest of our lives.

Right from the start, Stephan was a trooper! Everything had to have been brand new for him—riding in a car, being held by strangers, even wearing clothes that fit him—but besides an hour or so in the car where he got too hot and hungry and tired, he was a great sport as we ferried him all over town. He took to his stroller like a champ and ate everything I offered him and slept through the first night. We kept Stephan as close as we could to what we had been told had been his regular schedule and he went right along with it.

After the first night in the dumpy Hotel Russia, where we were all steaming in the humidity and noise (and I was awake every hour wondering if Stephan's little legs were getting stuck in the sides of the crib since there were no pillowy bumpers like most U.S. cribs had), we decided to get comfortable and move to the Marriott, where our room was cool and calm and lovely.

There was just one more paper to sign and an interview at the U.S. Embassy, which turned out to be more of a formality than anything else. Getting into the building was another matter—they dumped out my purse and examined the camera, my phone, our tape recorder, and my hairspray. And then we went through the metal detectors! While there, a stern but smiling Russian official scolded me and said, "And don't spoil him by picking him up when he cries!" Well, alrighty then, I thought, that was odd.

Still, when we exited the building, camera and hairspray and child in tow, Stephan was *ours!* Forever, permanently, no turning back now. No crazy Birth Mother to pop out of the woodwork or change her mind. At long, long, long last—I was someone's mom, mother to the sweetest, most beautiful little trooper of a boy on the entire planet.

But oh—then came the plane ride.

Pavarotti's Got Nothing on You...

I WAS GIDDY WITH EXCITEMENT, and was so, so (*so*) happy to be heading home with our beautiful little baby boy! Wait until my family got a load of this little gem—I felt like I had a gigantic ruby in my pocket, like there was nothing on earth that could touch the sense of richness I felt holding Stephan in my arms, of getting to march around on the planet with my new and long-coveted moniker of Stephan's mom.

We got to the Moscow airport with plenty of time to spare, I with my carefully packed and repacked baby bag in tow: numerous bottles of formula, aspirin, ear drops just in case (what the heck would Stephan think of flying when he'd barely even been out of doors?), that lovely blue traveling outfit courtesy of my friend Nancy and her family, two spare outfits just in case, countless diapers, blankies, bippies, bottles, crackers…you name it, I had it in triplicate.

Stephan's eyes were wide throughout the morning, but he remained mostly silent, intently watching and twisting his head to soak up everything all around him. As soon as we bid our farewells to our interpreter and gang—we were safely in the confines of the airport and had passed through all the visa and other official checkpoints—the trouble began.

I already knew Stephan's signs well enough to know when he needed a diaper change, so off I bustled towards the restroom, happy as a clam, a clean diaper in my purse, Stephan looking utterly adorable in his fancy blue outfit.

But when I got into the bathroom—oh my God, there had been an explosion! He had pooped all over his outfit, it had leaked out of his diaper, all down his pants, even covering the top of his outfit. There was no saving his clothing; I would have to give him a sort of bathroom sink bath and wrap him in his blankie and walk back to where David and our bags sat some way down the airport hallway and give him a new outfit there.

So I cooed and *oohed* and *aahed* as I cleaned up his tiny pink body as best I could, tossed the once-lovely blue outfit into the garbage, and swaddled Stephan up in his blankie—he looked nice and cozy!—to march him back down to our stuff for a full change of clothes.

As I walked the fifty or so yards down the sterile airport hallway towards the area where David sat, a seemingly unending parade of glaring *babushkas* passed me by, staring daggers at me, some even mumbling what I assumed were Russian profanities in my direction. I recalled how I had been told that in Russia they think that any and all child illnesses are caused by cold, so to see a child not overdressed to the point of sweating was apparently a huge social faux pas.

But I made it back to our area, got a change of clothes for Stephan, and shielded him as I redressed him.

Half an hour later, another explosion. Oh no, I had only one set of clothes left and we had twelve hours of travel ahead of us! Still, I had no choice but to hustle back down the long hallway and once again clean Stephan up and change him, hoping all the while that I wouldn't be tarred and feathered by any passing *babushkas.*

Eventually we were called for boarding, and I saw that there were at least a half-dozen other families traveling back to the States with their new babies as well. Phew, I thought—we won't be the only ones dealing with a baby seeing the world for the first time!

Once on board the plane—and we had requested and gotten seats with plenty of legroom—Stephan was a champ for the first half hour or so, but then he let loose.

It started as an "I'm angry and where the heck are you taking me?" cry. The cry turned into a wail. And once we were at cruising altitude, the wail turned into a screeching, angry, defiant, nonstop caterwaul.

I walked Stephan up and down the aisles, rocked him, sang to him, silently threatened him. Nothing quieted him. The other adoptees around the plane mostly slept or cooed quietly, but not our little Stephan. He cried, yelled, screamed, wailed, shot daggers at us with his eyes. This tiny little being was pissed off, angry as hell, and I'm sure terrified as well, and he was not shy about letting us know it.

I thought his lungs would burst right out of his little body. How could something so tiny make such a huge amount of noise?

"He's cute as hell but has lungs like Pavarotti," I muttered to myself as a stewardess tried rocking him. She was Russian, maybe she knew something about Russian babies I didn't? She rocked him so hard, with violent shakes from right to left, wide arcs, then left to right. *Jesus, he's just a tiny baby, what is it with these Russians and their toughness?* I thought as I grabbed him back.

David had a look on his face that was both hilarious and alarming, as though he would have preferred a parachute to twenty more seconds of Stephan's wailing.

But despite the fact that Stephan's defiant, pissed-off shrieking likely permed the hair of all the folks around us, despite the fact that for ten hours straight I walked and rocked and constantly moved with a squalling Stephan in my arms, we finally touched down in New York City, the United States, the good old U.S. of A.

We were all exhausted, and Stephan hung limp in his carrier, wrung out, still pissed off, but finally quiet.

We were home!

III. Home

Home in Brooklyn

May 25

BLISS. JET LAG. Exhaustion. Elation. I was Stephan's mom, and I felt inherently rich, as though I was secretly carrying a priceless gemstone in my pocket.

We had made it through the final endless flight from Moscow back to New York City, Stephan screaming bloody murder the entire time—and when I say the entire time, I do not mean he napped for thirty minutes here or there or stopped somewhere over Greenland to catch his breath. By the time we finally got off the plane, with me carrying Stephan in the baby harness across my chest, his little arms and legs hanging limp and wan, his face pallid, his eyes red from screaming—I knew he was exhausted, wrung out, and I was as well.

Still, we made it home and started to feather the nest for our new family.

That first night at home, after some cursory unpacking and wandering around in jet-lagged circles, a few hours later I went to put Stephan down in his brand-new, very own crib. I loved the happy yellow sheets I had carefully picked out and that I had tucked in just so, the bumper around the edges to ensure that his limbs would be safe and not get stuck between the wooden slats. I smiled and kissed Stephan and laid him down in his brand-new bed, murmuring, "Welcome home, love."

Stephan exploded.

He wailed, yowled, screeched, protested. It was as if I had laid him down on a bed of hot coals. I recalled the odd Russian doctor in one of the many embassies we had had to pass through who had said, "Don't spoil him, let him know that you're in charge," which I knew was mostly malarkey but nonetheless had stuck with me. I let Stephan cry for a few minutes—I am not proud to say it—and then picked him up. He stopped crying. We walked around, he looked exhausted, I put him down once more—again the wailing began. I quickly left his room and thought, Please, dear God, just give me my bed…just an hour. Twenty minutes, I'll take twenty minutes! I just want, I *need*, to shut my eyes…

Wahhhhh! Stephan seemed to give his wail an extra blast, maybe just to get my attention. I waited a beat, inhaled deeply, and went back into his room and picked him up. His cries slowed to a whimper. We walked slowly in circles in his small room. He stopped screaming as we walked. The third time I put him down, I was so exhausted myself that I couldn't think straight, didn't know if I could even hold him any longer securely in my arms.

I let Stephan yowl for a minute and then called my mom in Los Angeles.

"I'm so exhausted, he cries no matter what, he's crying in his perfect little crib—should I pick him up?" My brain was as curdled as cottage cheese.

Like any sane, kind, experienced mother she said, "Yes, go pick him up this minute!"

So I picked up Stephan and he stopped crying. I knew he must have been utterly freaked out; virtually everything he had ever known had changed in the last forty-eight hours. Everything that surrounded him, I thought, was new, unfamiliar, foreign, and probably very scary. The language and sounds he was hearing, the smells, the food, the bed, *me,* the background noises, the weather, every bit of his surroundings—nothing was the same. I knew that anger was the flip side of fear, and in my occasional lucid, non-exhausted moments, I imagined how terrified Stephan must be to have been feeling so enraged.

I totally understood in my adult, logical mind why Stephan was so upset, but after forty-eight sleepless hours, with his screeching and hurling himself around, my mind was a gray blur.

I looked into his exhausted but beautiful face, into his hazel eyes, at his tiny perfect chin. He cracked an almost smile. Pinch me, I am home and am the mother of a beautiful, sweet, strong-willed little boy. No crazy pregnant lady can come and take him away or ask me to do another personality test or clarify what happened when I was eleven years old—my little Stephan was mine and we were home!

I hugged his little exhausted, angry body, assured us both that I loved him and our family forever and was so, so, so thrilled to be home together. At last.

I think we passed out on the couch, Stephan leaning against my chest, his exhausted, shallow baby breaths pressing against my heart. I had surrendered to his tiny self, his small but dominating presence, to our mutual love, our mutual exhaustion, our breath. I woke up sometime later and gently put Stephan into his crib, where he finally spent a first few peaceful moments in seemingly deep sleep.

Morning Number One

Home in Brooklyn, morning number 1

THE BLACK LIGHT TURNED to blue, then slowly to golden pink outside my window, and as I rolled over and opened my eyes more fully, I knew it was morning. A lovely spring morning.

It had been a rough night—after a brief sleep when I had first put him in his crib, Stephan wailed on and off for hours, and with such ferocity that at one point I couldn't help but wonder if he could hurt himself by screaming so hard, his face flushed, his eyes bulging with the effort. I also had to admit that, the fourth or fifth time I had gotten up in the night, the question had crossed my sleepless, delirious mind: Had I made the right decision or were the rest of my days and nights going to be spent trying to console a seemingly inconsolable little boy?

I had grabbed bits of sleep here and there, but never enough to go down deep or get really rested; when I saw the sun outside the window and the morning's golden light, I wondered for a minute where I was. Was I in Russia? Was our scowling Siberian adoption representative waiting in the lobby with more threats? I rubbed my eyes and looked around. No, no… I was home, home in bed in Brooklyn. With Stephan.

I tiptoed towards Stephan's room and checked to make sure that I hadn't dreamt the whole thing—phew, Stephan was still there! Despite his near-constant distress during the night, he had never wanted to get into bed with me—right from the start, he seemed to like having his own space.

He jolted awake as soon as he heard the door crack open. "Hello, sweet boy," I said and picked him up gently. He was warm and moist and pink and so very little. I sat us down in the rocking chair and pulled open the curtain on the window that overlooked the garden two floors below.

"Look, that's your tree, see how big it is? And down there is a deck with a table on it, we can go out there later if it's nice out..." Stephan's eyes were as wide as saucers as he took in the view; the leaves, the sky, the sound of a dog barking in the distance. He did seem amenable to distraction, so at least we had that going for us.

We made it through the day, going from juice and squishy food to changing diapers, playing with soft toys, reading *Goodnight Moon*, lying on the couch in exhaustion. Day turned to afternoon, the sky darkened, night fell. As much as I yearned for sleep, I dreaded bedtime, whenever that might come. I thought, Stephan has only been home for two days and he already has me as trained as Pavlov's dog—whenever I put him in bed and left the room, my body tensed and my heart quickened as I braced for the inevitable explosion that I knew would come.

That evening, as I rocked Stephan in the chair and sang to him—optimistically hoping that all the new sights and experiences he had enjoyed would cause such happy exhaustion that he would pass right out—I thought of what David's stepmother had said in her Long Island drawl, "Aww, you're going to need help with the baby." Me? Nah, not me, I had said. One tiny little baby? I'm not like that side of the family, concerned about china patterns and being seen at the right restaurants, the social-climbing factor that I somehow connected to assuming one needed a nanny when one had just one tiny little baby.

I don't need help, I had said with certainty. My own mom had said, "Ah, you'll be fine—feed him, change him, love him, and make sure you have plenty of wine around!"

That night was a repeat of the night before—little to no sleep, angry wailing from Stephan, David out of town as usual so it was just me and my little screaming boy.

I knew that all new parents go through sleepless nights, but when you are in the midst of it, you can't think straight at all, you don't know if it is day or night, and furthermore you don't *care* if it is day or night—you just want sleeeeep. Beautiful, tranquil, quiet, wake-up-refreshed sleep.

By day three, neither Stephan nor I had had a decent night's sleep. Or a good daytime nap. I started to think that maybe I could use some help—perhaps just a few daytime hours so I could get some sleep and make it through the long nights? Yes, that might be the ticket…

By day four, as sleepless and hellish as the preceding days had been, suddenly the exhaustion overtook Stephan's terror and rage and he fell deeply asleep. Oh, how angelic his little face looked while he slept! His tiny features, his cherubic cheeks, his perfect golden curly locks, his pursed lips, quietly inhaling and exhaling while his tiny eyelids fluttered. I hoped he was having sweet dreams.

The next morning I awoke knowing that Stephan was in the next room and I was in—bliss. Amazing how sleep can totally alter and readjust your perspective; Stephan was slowly learning to trust me, to recognize my face and listen for me, and he gave me the biggest grin yet when I opened his door and said, "Good morning, sweet boy."

We spent the day strolling through town with a neighbor and her daughter, Stephan leaning forward in his stroller, us laughing together, me talking to him nonstop, his body so tiny at nine months old that the toes at the ends of his outstretched legs didn't even reach the end of the stroller's seat cushion. He looked sweetly comical, leaning forward like a race car driver looking for the next turn, his eyes expectant and wide as he took it all in. The cars, a cat, a stop sign, other people, a bookstore! I could almost see the little gears in his head racing a million miles an hour—compared to the gray doldrums of the orphanage in Russia, never going out of doors, what his hospital stay must have been like during his first six months of life, it was as though he had suddenly entered a Technicolor Alice in Wonderland–style funhouse!

Everywhere we turned there was something brand new, enchanting, perhaps scary. A tree, a girl, a barking dog, a grocery store with loud music and bright lights and multicolored boxes surrounding us on all sides.

I was constantly high on Stephan's expression of wonderment but also aware of how easily overloaded he could be, so I was wary of big crowds or doing too many things at once. I nixed the idea of our traveling way out to Long Island for a baby shower at David's work—I imagined how terrified Stephan might be amidst a giant circle of cheering and drinking grownups!

I was utterly kid-drunk and loved every single one of Stephan's growing number of expressions, and now that I was getting a few minutes sleep, I was reveling in it all—the simplicity of sleep, eat, poo, walk, eat, sleep, poo. I had never been happier.

I loved being a mom 10,000 times more than I had ever thought possible. I rented my mom a sweet little sublet apartment for three months and she came to spend the summer with us, which would be absolutely amazing, especially since David was usually away working.

My job was starting to ask when I would return to the office. Mind you, our independent company had just been purchased by an international behemoth, and I'd been promised a promotion, a windowed corner office on Times Square—they wanted me back! Of course, it was extremely unappealing that I had been granted one (yes *one*) paid day of maternity leave since Stephan hadn't been ripped from my loins, in which case I would have gotten disability, which passes for maternity leave in this country. Naturally, these days no company could suggest such a thing but at that point I was too kid-drunk to fight it.

I suppose I had imagined that I would be conflicted about going back to work post-baby; I had always planned to go back, and for the most part I liked my job working for a music publisher, marketing out their music to TV commercials, movies, etc. How could I just turn away?

But every morning or when Stephan woke up from his nap and I was standing there and he recognized me and gave me a *huge* grin, I knew that nothing—nothing—could compare to that.

I beamed when we walked down the street, absolutely certain that I was the luckiest, most blessed, most slap-happy woman/mom on the planet (what, only *this* planet?).

Work couldn't hold a candle to that.

Kid-Drunk and Delirious

AS KID-DRUNK AS I WAS, and as elated as I felt to be a new mom, I was of course far from perfect.

Stephan had an iron will and a very definite personality. When he was unhappy, you knew it. I muttered more than once under my breath, after hours of nighttime screaming, "Shut up!" something about which I felt totally ashamed. I apologized profusely and told Stephan that I loved him unconditionally and forever, no matter what, and that I wasn't perfect but I would always do my best.

Man, could he wail! I knew all babies did but I was convinced that Stephan's wailing was the anguished and brain-piercing wail of the perennially underfed and unheld. The Pavlovian button for him may have been an empty tummy, which might mean in his brain possible death. He was, to put it mildly, most dramatic.

But man, how I loved every little piece of him!

Luckily, my mom—who was staying a mile or so away in a sublet apartment—had a magical effect on Stephan. She was a great natural teacher (as well as being a retired actual teacher) without being instructive and she could quiet and amaze Stephan like no one else.

A few days after we arrived home from Russia and Stephan and I had logged at least a bit of sleep, we had an appointment with pediatrician Dr. Aronson so she could give him a thorough physical exam and see just what may lie in store.

Dr. Aronson's office was on the Upper East Side of Manhattan, and as we lived many miles away in Park Slope, Brooklyn, I made the first of what would become frequent long subway trips solo with Stephan and stroller.

I figured I should leave at least an hour earlier than our appointment time, maybe an hour and a half, and left our house that morning with Stephan dressed in a cute outfit and tucked into his stroller, marched up our street two long blocks, then turned left onto Seventh Avenue and went four blocks to the subway stop. All the while, Stephan's tiny head was looking all around, craning left and right, taking in every sound, sight, and presumably smell. What an amazing brand-new world this must be to him, I constantly marveled, and through his expression was myself seeing everything in a refreshed and exciting new light.

A fire engine roared past, lights whirling, siren blaring. Stephan's eyes were huge! Then a woman walked by with seven dogs on leashes, big ones, small ones, furry ones, short-haired ones—I thought Stephan's eyes might burst right out of his head.

Once the excitement had passed and we were at the subway stop, I picked up the stroller to carry it downstairs to the subway platform. The first flight was about twenty stairs, then we turned a corner, then another twenty stairs.

Once at the bottom, we were on the platform. Stephan's expression was a mixture of fear and wonder as the sounds of an incoming train grew louder. "Look, here comes a train," I said and knelt down next to him. It was a pretty terrifying sensory experience—we had climbed a long way down below the ground into a dark and smelly tunnel where people milled around, some looking nervous, others dangerous, and where a giant, thundering electric snake sped directly at us, fierce red and yellow headlights as its eyes.

If Stephan could have screamed and run away, the look on his face made me imagine that he might. "It's okay, Scoop," I cooed, "that's the subway train." I'm not sure why or when I started calling Stephan Scoop, but he was gaining more nicknames with every passing day.

By the time that train pulled out and he watched its taillights disappear into the tunnel, Stephan looked more amazed and curious than scared.

Soon our train came banging into the station, the doors slid open, people jostled out, and I picked up the stroller to get into the car. People looked towards Stephan and smiled—he was so tiny, his expression so intense, so vivid! His body was itty-bitty, the soles of his tiny sock-clad feet pointing in whatever direction we were heading.

I thought he was the absolute cutest, most beautiful, most perfect, most irresistible little baby the world had ever seen, and nothing could or would ever convince me otherwise. I swelled with pride, pushing the stroller and knowing he was my baby. My son. Yep, I still felt like I was cradling that gemstone in my pocket and soul and nothing and no one could touch the feeling.

With every stop, the train would screech to a halt, the doors would slide open, and bodies would pack on and off the train. Stephan's eyes were wide with awe every second of the journey, and each time the train doors hissed closed and the train lurched back up to speed, he would look at me with an "Isn't this incredible?" expression that made me laugh.

We made it to Union Station, where we transferred to an uptown subway; we got off of our train, went up two flights of stairs, across a platform, and then back down two flights of stairs to catch the next one. Stephan wasn't heavy—at nine months old, he still weighed only about as much as a healthy American newborn—but the stroller was awkward and when we got onto the uptown train, I was happy to grab a seat and hold the stroller in front of me.

A few minutes later, it was our uptown stop. Off the train we went—and this station was weirdly far underground, more so than any other one I had been in—then up the longest escalator I had ever seen. Up, up, up it went, seemingly forever, and I couldn't help but imagine that it was like ascending from the depths of Hell.

Once we went up at least a fifty-yard stretch of escalator, we crossed another platform and then we went up two flights of stairs.

Phew, at last, back into daylight!

Stephan blinked his little eyes hard in the bright spring sunshine and I shielded his face with my hand to give him a minute to adjust. And then off I pushed his stroller the few blocks to Dr. Aronson's office.

Dr. Aronson's office was on the bottom floor of what looked like an old brownstone that had been converted to professional space, and it retained a homey, welcoming air. When we were called into the exam room, Dr. Aronson asked me about him. Without thinking I said, "He's tough." Then added, "Sweet but tough."

Dr. Aronson commenced to poke and prod and draw blood from Stephan so she could do tests for any diseases, blood issues, anemia, etc.

"I'm going to have to draw blood from his neck for this one so hold onto him tight," Dr. Aronson said matter-of-factly. I grabbed Stephan firmly but gently and held on to him and before I could ask why the neck, she had deftly stuck a needle into his tiny pink neck and taken the blood sample she needed.

Stephan was more surprised than anything and was huffing, his eyes bulging in a "How could you let her do this to me?" expression, but he had not yet cried.

"Wow, he is tough," the doctor smiled.

Happily, there was nothing obviously wrong with Stephan, and Dr. Aronson diagnosed him in general as okay but needing lots more testing, and recommended we get him tested for any early intervention needs.

"What's early intervention?" I asked innocently.

The doctor told me that lots, if not most kids who had come from international orphanages where they lacked adequate food or medical care or attention, had absent learning (simply put, they hadn't always had the normal range of experiences a typical healthy and well-tended baby would have had, whether it was being spoken or sung to, carried around to places out of doors, seeing animals, reaching for toys or a bottle, etc.) and had not developed like their peers. Dr. Aronson said they called it "failure to thrive," a very broad term for having missed out on the usual prenatal care, postnatal care, and early infancy development, aka having been ignored and lacking mental and/or physical growth and development on a "normal" scale.

"Sure, that sounds great," I said as I took the paper with the names and numbers her nurse had scrawled out for me.

Little did I know.

He Understand Notting

I CONTINUED TO STALL THINGS with my job—it was tempting to go back (that corner office overlooking Times Square was very sexy and impressive except that Stephan wouldn't be there), but the notion of leaving Stephan for an entire day was something that was for me still very much in the realm of future possibilities, never in the *now*. I mean, I even missed him when he was asleep! Although the days and nights were exhausting and nonstop, they were even more heavenly, awe-filled, and irreplaceable.

Thus far motherhood was intense, wonderful, difficult, heavenly, exasperating; the highs of his smile when he awoke from a nap, the lows of his defiant screeching when he wanted something and I hadn't slept since I could remember.

I told my job that I needed to take (unpaid) family leave for three months, figuring that would buy me some time to see how I felt about going back to work.

BY July, Stephan had grown and changed so much since he had come home in May. He had gone from an anxious, skinny, scared, hungry little orphan waif to an increasingly happy, confident, playful, giggly little dude. He actually outgrew some of his clothes!

As Dr. Aronson had suggested, I called a few numbers and soon was met by a bevy of child development specialists, each of whom came to our house to individually evaluate Stephan. I watched as each person played with Stephan, held him, watched him, gently test-ed his baby reflexes and abilities. I was bursting with pride—wasn't he beautiful? Look at that face! I could see he was small and stiff but in my eyes he was otherwise absolutely perfect.

A short time later I got the written evaluation and it was rec-ommended that Stephan should receive early intervention in every possible category: physical therapy, occupational therapy, special education, and speech therapy. I was slightly taken aback—was Stephan really that far off base from the "norm?"—but, as ignorance was bliss, I didn't think too hard about it. Whatever my boy needed, I would make sure he got!

It was also recommended that, as Stephan apparently under-stood little or no English at the level a "normal" child of his age would, we should have a Russian speaker come and see if he respond-ed to that language.

A stern and elegant young Russian woman shortly came to our house, played with Stephan, and chit-chatted quietly. I remember she held up a Russian doll and repeated a word, seeing if he knew it or could repeat it. Stephan remained silent.

Afterwards she turned to me and said slowly in that so-easily-mocked, super-thick Russian accent, "He understand *notting.*"

I smiled and nodded—had no one spoken to him at all? What about at the hospital? What about the orphanage? No one had held him, sung to him? Maybe they didn't have time since he was sickly and had been premature and they had their hands more than full with the kids who were healthy enough to survive a rough situation.

Alright, let's go, I thought, *he'll catch up in no time!* I asked for and was given a pages-long list of early intervention therapists in the Brooklyn area.

Welcome to the World of
Early Intervention

LOOKING BACK, IT IS just as well that I had no idea: (a) how deep and broad Stephan's physical, developmental, and experiential deficits and thus needs really were; and (b) just what a gigantic and ongoing commitment it would take from us both, but mostly from him.

When I looked at Stephan, I saw a beautiful, willful, mega-determined, tiny, sweet, and responsive little boy, all of which he definitely was (and is). When each early intervention therapist looked at him from the perspectives of their various specialties, they apparently saw something utterly different and very real: a baby boy desperate for help in every area and one who had been deprived of so many of the essential things that make for a healthy and happy start in life. He had had zero prenatal care, having been a hidden pregnancy. And who knew what that really meant? Did his birth mother drink so no one would think she was pregnant? Did she do any minimal curtailing of her usual activities that pregnant woman might normally do or did she just let it rip? And as importantly, what was her emotional state? Was she hating his being there inside of her? Or did she secretly love him and wish him well?

Given the information I had about Stephan and his journey in life to that point, I couldn't help but imagine his Birth Mother trying to get rid of him—steep stairs, vigorous exercise, radically inappropriate diet?—though I certainly hoped that wasn't the case. But I couldn't shake it from my mind, especially as time went on, that the very initial germination of Stephan's life was into an unwelcome time and an unwelcome place, so much so that his very existence was denied. I have since thought, in the moments I let myself go down that dark road, that he has always carried the branding of that unwelcome feeling deep in his marrow.

But then I think, oh, what the hell…we're both sultry and emotional Russians, Stephan and I, and that whole melancholy, deep-thinking soulful thing rings absolutely true.

It's partly the seemingly endless Russian winters—if you've ever flown from Moscow to Siberia in the winter and been awed by the hours and hours of flat white space constantly unfolding below you, the prehistoric, timeless, humbling feeling that washes over you, you know what I mean. But it's more than that—there is a depth that that particular kind of endless deep cold and time and vastness of space breeds into the Russian soul (to which I feel very attached and proud of, for better or worse), and it defies national boundaries and era. It is a yearning, lonely, enlightened, confident, lost kind of compass, but one I have always felt and truly recognized as Russian when I went there. And one that Stephan definitely owns as well (as does my mother). I am proud to bear it, and would not feel myself without it, this cold, bright, steely-strong, lonely Russian heart, though it is not a light load.

Anyway, even years later, it still opens a searing raw nerve for me to stop and contemplate the possibilities of what Stephan's very first days and weeks were like, and how his very vulnerable, needy, and sensitive baby soul somehow survived by sheer grit and stubbornness.

We are not talking about a preemie born in the U.S., in L.A.'s Cedars–Sinai Hospital perhaps, with a Birth Mother/Birth Parents playing Beethoven sonatas on her tummy, with some of the best doctors in the world guiding and testing and aiding her, with an internationally top-level Neonatal Intensive Care Unit monitoring and supporting the baby every step of the way.

Not only had Stephan been a hidden pregnancy, but he was born about two months prematurely (I couldn't help but imagine that might have been due to some prodding, but I hoped I was wrong) and then left in a hospital to fend for himself. He weighed about two pounds at birth and had pneumonia. I can only hope that some kindly nurse had a soft spot for him—the nurses who work in NICUs are often absolute angels—and sometimes rocked him or otherwise gave him warm comfort.

Despite my darker moments, I have always believed, as I still do today, that for a Birth Mother to relinquish her child if she knows she cannot parent him or her well, or perhaps even at all, is a supreme act of love and courage. I cannot fathom making such a choice and deeply admire those who can and do, including Stephan's Birth Mother, wherever she may be. I told Stephan as much as soon as he was old enough to understand, having always been very open and proud about how we found each other and became a family.

And so there we were, suddenly but inevitably a family, Stephan having survived against the odds to have made his debut on planet Earth and then all the way to infancy, I having surfed my way through some disastrously horrifying and hilarious misadventures in my quest to become a mother. Perhaps we had been brought together by the wicked black humor of fate, we two little terriers who had gotten hold of a notion we were unwilling to let go of—both of us aimed for family, and I think meant to find each other.

When I looked at Stephan, even later when he was nose to nose with one of his numerous therapists, I saw only his shine, his drive, his unbelievable strength, his possibilities, all the things the world had in store for him and he for it. Of course, I soon began to understand how much work lay ahead of him—he was going to have to use every bit of physical and mental strength to learn to crawl, to form intentional sounds, to be able to move his arms, his legs, his lips, in deliberate ways. Eventually I came to understand how each amazing therapist saw him, and how much work they knew he had to do, and how they could affect his life, both then and in the future.

But in those early days, I saw Stephan as a glowing little bundle of promise—had he or I known what lay ahead, the knowledge might have made the journey too daunting to begin. I only understood later how essential that blissfully ignorant perspective was to us both.

Tasia

AFTER I HAD GONE THROUGH long lists of early intervention providers close to our Brooklyn neighborhood—speech therapists, special educators (whatever that meant), physical therapists (how could you do physical therapy on an infant?), and occupational therapy (what, were they going to teach Stephan welding?)—I set appointments for our first few sessions.

Little did I know, the amazing, gifted, generous women who were about to enter our lives were to permanently alter the trajectory of Stephan's life and open my eyes to a whole new world.

I can't remember which therapist came first, who showed up in our small Brooklyn living room with a bag of baby toys and temptations, and who quickly got down on the ground and started manipulating, teaching, and sometimes torturing my little Stephan.

Each and every one of them was a miracle, full of love and tenacity and brilliant skills.

Tasia was our special ed therapist and an absolute godsend. She was one of those people whom you see doing their work and it is obviously also their passion and *raison d'être*, and you find yourself saying, "Wow, now that is someone who loves her job, and thank goodness she's doing it in my world!" Tasia, who was probably in her late twenties and had swinging brown hair and an easy smile, showed up for every appointment with an overstuffed bag of toys and goodies, then plopped down on the living room floor across from Stephan.

Her task was a more general one than some of the other therapists, which was both vaguer and perhaps more challenging (and I later discovered that special ed teachers get paid significantly less than some of the other E.I. teachers, so not fair). She was to engage with Stephan on every level and try to get a sense of what he lacked (everything!), and start to fill in those gaps with play, reading, interaction, and positivity.

Tasia would chit-chat merrily with Stephan and quickly found out what toys and games most piqued his interest. It was definitely cars. Cars and Elmo. She knew just how to entice Stephan out of passive mode, and in retrospect I feel like I got, not only from her but all of Stephan's therapists, a hands-on degree in early childhood development.

And to Stephan's credit, he quickly learned, and I think often even enjoyed, the one-on-one time with each therapist. He had never gotten any attention that we could tell, hadn't crawled, hadn't been out of doors, likely hadn't been cooed or *oohed* or *aahed* over. And so he quickly learned how to lean in, literally, to be attentive and on task, and little by little showed just how much grit he really possessed.

Typically, Tasia would come in, settle cross-legged on the floor, Stephan propped up across from her on a bevy of large soft pillows (it took a while for him to have the strength to hold himself up physically), and select a toy. I remember one of Stephan's favorites was a plastic garage that held four or five cars that you could make pop out of the various doors.

Tasia would move slowly and deliberately and shove all the other toys out of sight so Stephan could more easily focus. She would make her eyes big as she slowly held up the chosen toy. "Wwwooooow..." she would say. Stephan would mirror her, his little eyes growing wider, and then lean in and reach for the toy. Tasia would gently hold it just out of his reach, and then say to Stephan, "Give me," while patting her open palm on her chest, sign language for "give it to me." I think the first few times she physically took Stephan's tiny little one-year-old hand and showed him how to make the motion. And then she gave him the toy.

I get emotional even remembering these moments, when Stephan first realized that he could have some power and control over his world, at least by asking for things. It did not take long, not more than one session if I remember correctly, before Stephan was motioning "Give me" and then beaming with pride when whatever coveted object was handed to him.

Tasia took obvious joy in each and every little or big hurdle that Stephan overcame. He would reach for one of the cars in the little plastic garage but Tasia would cover the "open" button. "Open," she would say clearly, "open." It took weeks and months before Stephan was comfortable even trying to mouth any words—he had rarely cooed or babbled and had to that point never really attempted to form specific sounds or words, something a normally developing infant likely does between nine months and a year. It was a few more months before we realized that Stephan had major issues with speech, but I will get to that later. But the great thing was that he was always game to keep trying.

Tasia would repeat the word "open," and then remove her hand for Stephan to again hit the button, Tasia sometimes needing to help him apply enough pressure to get the thing to open. She always did it with a smile, with sweet encouragement, and with a sense of awe when Stephan had taken any action to make something happen.

Her hand on top of his, they pushed the "open" button and the door popped open and a little plastic car rolled out.

"Ta-da!" Tasia laughed happily. Stephan looked up at her and smiled, clearly enjoying the moment. Then he put the car back into the door, wanting to work that same magic again.

"Again?" Tasia would laugh. "More?" When she said "more," she would bunch the fingers of each hand together and then tap the fingertips together in front of her, the sign for "more." "More," she would say slowly, tapping her bunched fingers, and then reaching over to gently mold Stephan's tiny pink hands into the same motion and tap them together. Tap, tap, "More..." Stephan caught on quickly and was thrilled to open the door, tap his fingers together for "more," stuff the car back into the little garage, and hit the button once again.

Stephan's attention never wavered, and towards the end of each session, which was both mentally and physically exhausting for him, Tasia would pull out a book and end with a sweet story. As weeks and months passed, Stephan came to have certain favorite books, including *Goodnight Moon,* and Tasia would sometimes hold up two books to let him choose. Stephan was clearly a boy who liked to choose and took great joy in learning all the various ways he could be in control of the world around him, even in the small ways typical of an infant and then toddler.

The days turned to weeks and then months, the seasons changed—sometimes Tasia would show up soaking wet from a downpour, others sweating from walking from the subway in the summer heat. Her smiling face and loving demeanor always graced our home and to this day, I tear up thinking about how much love and learning she poured into Stephan and our lives.

But there was one moment in particular that I will never forget and that let us know, without any doubt, that Stephan was one smart cookie with a very linear and sharp mind. We called it the Chicken Moment.

The Chicken Moment

THE CHICKEN MOMENT OCCURRED on one of the days that Tasia came to our house for a session with Stephan.

Right from the start, Stephan was seeing each of his four therapists two or three times a week, and he had sessions twice a day. So a typical day went something like this: wake up, have breakfast, maybe go for a brief stroll if the weather was nice, then the first session of the day would start at around ten or eleven A.M. The session would last more or less fort-five minutes (there is only so long you can expect a baby or toddler to be attentive), the therapist would leave, and Stephan and I would have a snack, and maybe he'd take a nap or otherwise relax. Then in the afternoon around two or so, the second therapist of the day would arrive. This was our routine four to five days a week, which was a lot for anyone, but especially for a small and underdeveloped baby. But as I have said, to his amazing credit, not once—ever—did Stephan turn away from the work before him.

So one day Tasia was at our house, cross-legged on the floor across from little Stephan, who at that point was just learning how and getting the strength to crawl. He must have been about a year and a half old. Tasia pulled out of her bag a book about farm animals. Stephan loved animals, especially dogs and cats, and was fascinated by the book.

I sat, as always, a foot or two away behind Stephan so I could observe without being distracting. I was also learning, with every second of every session, how these experts instructed and cajoled and worked with Stephan to help him make up for all the developmental and experiential time he had missed.

Tasia opened to the first page. "'Moo,' said the cow," she read. "'Moo.'" Stephan leaned forward and touched the book. Tasia slowly turned the page. "'Baaa,' said the sheep. 'Baaa.'" Stephan looked at me as if to say, "Isn't this amazing, isn't this great?" "Baaa," I repeated, and Stephan smiled.

Tasia turned the page. "'Cluck,' said the chicken," Tasia said. Suddenly Stephan sat up straighter and his eyes widened. It was as clear an "aha" lightbulb moment as you would see in a cartoon. Stephan leaned forward and began to commando crawl towards the stairs. (He was too weak at that point to crawl on all fours, so he would pull himself forward with his bent arms, his weight resting on his elbows, his weak legs mostly dragging limp behind him like a soldier in the underbrush.)

"What's he doing?" I asked with a laugh.

"He's looking for a chicken," Tasia said.

"Ha, that's funny!" I laughed. "We don't have any chickens in this house! No chicken stuffed animals, no books about chickens—I am sure that this is a chicken-free area!"

But Stephan seemed to know exactly where he was headed, and Tasia had the good sense to follow him and let him keep going, with me a step behind them.

Stephan started up the stairs, a very laborious task, with Tasia supporting him from behind, and he somehow pulled and crawled his way upstairs and towards his room, his little face beaming with determination and excitement the whole way.

In his small room, Stephan made a beeline for his little toy chest, opened the lid, and started rummaging around.

"Yep, he is definitely looking for a chicken," Tasia laughed. I stood in the doorway, sure there were no chickens to be found.

Stephan leaned into the wooden chest as far as he could and got hold of something. He struggled to pull it out and Tasia bent down to help him. Stephan pulled out a wooden toy he had recently been given, a handmade board with a picture of a farm painted on it, with eight or ten hinged windows that opened to reveal individual wooden figures of various animals. There was a cow, a dog, a horse, a sheep, etc.

Without hesitating, Stephan pulled open one specific window and grabbed the little wooden animal figure inside. He held it up in his tiny hand with a "ta-da!" expression on his grinning face.

Tasia leaned in to take a look. "It's a chicken!" she laughed. "Wow, great job, Stephan!"

I stood there amazed—I had never seen that chicken, we had never played together with that toy, and I had certainly never said the word "chicken" specifically to Stephan.

"What the…?" I said.

Tasia turned towards me with a very satisfied grin. "He's going to be just fine," she said.

"How on earth did he do that?" I laughed.

We let Stephan proudly wave his wooden chicken around in his fist, and then Tasia carried him back downstairs to finish their session.

When the session was over and Tasia was packing up her bag of toys, Stephan relaxing with a sippy cup, she said, "I'd rather see him do that than be able to say 'A, B, C.'" I had no response. "He is putting it all together, and that is something that I cannot teach him how to do."

There was so much that Stephan's Chicken Moment had revealed—his memory, his ability to identify specific shapes and concepts, his linear thinking, the ability to connect from the present to the past, not to mention his physical determination (as if that had ever been in question).

"Good job today, Stephan," Tasia said, and gave him a baby-sized high five.

When Tasia had gone on her way to the next client and another child whose life would potentially be changed and definitely enriched by her amazing gift and talent, I looked at my little Stephan with renewed pride and curiosity. Just what exactly was churning away in that fertile mind of his? I knew the wheels of his mind were turning like mad, he was a tiny mega-sponge, starved to absorb as much of the world as possible, and often, as in the Chicken Moment, he was amazing me and everyone around him with his resiliency and smarts.

Poo

AH, I REMEMBER the poo years.

Seriously, there were probably at least three months—that's nine-ty separate days—where I had to collect Stephan's poo on a daily basis, mix it into a tube, stick it in the fridge, and later run it down a few blocks to the local lab.

Dr. Aronson had suggested that Stephan be tested for every-thing: rickets, anemia, measles, parasites, blood diseases, liver prob-lems, etc., many of which had been listed on his medical card in the orphanage and were also likely to live in someone of his background. And so I diligently collected every needed sample, used the round, flat popsicle stick provided by the lab, smeared it into the relevant test tube, secured the tube in a sealed envelope, put that envelope into a bag, and then walked the bag to the lab drop-off.

The good news was that, despite all the possibly dire predictions, all the concern whether he might have had or still carried a dreaded disease, of whether he might have some serious, chronic illness due to his very neglected, sick start in life, Stephan seemed to be mainly okay.

It was also recommended that we get Stephan's eyes checked, specifically his corneal pressure, since apparently a lot of preemies have low eye pressure and that can lead to poor vision along with many other issues.

The pediatric eye doctor we were sent to had some very specialized equipment that let him test a baby's retinal pressure. When I trekked with Stephan to his office—it was deep in a residential, non-hip neighborhood of Brooklyn—the waiting room was chock-full of mothers and strollers and screaming toddlers. Man, I did not envy the receptionist.

When it was our turn, the doctor looked into Stephan's eyes in all the usual ways, then told me he would need to dilate his pupils, have us wait for an hour or so, and then come back for him to retest the pressure. So after the doctor dropped the dilating liquid into Stephan's eyes, I put him back into his stroller and we left to walk around the neighborhood for a while.

I made sure the shade cover was down over Stephan's head, and he may even have had on baby-sized dark cardboard glasses. Forty or so minutes later, we went back to the office and the doctor used a gauge to measure Stephan's eye pressure.

"Wow," he said when he stood back up.

"What?" I asked with alarm. "Is everything okay?"

"He's got the best retinal pressure I've ever seen in a preemie," the doctor said.

"Hah! That's my boy," I smiled.

I couldn't help but feel proud of Stephan, though of course I had nothing to do with his retinal pressure. I felt proud of him for his survival skills, for being tough as nails although tiny, and for putting up with so much prodding and examining without ever crying or complaining or turning away.

Leann

THROUGH IT ALL, every day Stephan was growing a bit bigger
and a bit stronger and a bit less freaked out. By his first birthday, he
was making giant leaps; he would go to sleep on his back in my arms
rather than face towards me against my chest. He weighed almost
seventeen pounds and was twenty inches tall.

And the early intervention continued. Leann was our physical
therapist, another wonderful teacher and instructor who brought
so much to our lives.

Leann began by, in essence, trying to unlock Stephan's tightly
wound and unmuscled limbs. Here was a baby who had apparently
never crawled or moved or pulled himself to a stand like most babies
love to do. He could hardly roll over and when he did, his body
moved in one tiny, "heave-ho" kind of lurch, as though he were a very
determined little pink two-by-four. His stomach was still distended
when Leann began working with Stephan at about a year old, partly
from malnutrition, partly from lack of "muscle tone" (or as those in
the E.I. world called it, "low muscle tone").

Leann had ways of getting Stephan to challenge himself physically without realizing he was doing it. For example, she would hold a
red Elmo doll just out of his reach, and Stephan would lean towards
it and try to grab it. Depending on what part of his body Leann was
working on, she would restrict or direct Stephan physically. She'd
get him to reach to the left across his body with his right arm while

she was gently holding his hips and legs in place on the floor so he would have to flex his stiff hip muscles. She had all kinds of ways to get him to bend and flex and move. Some of it looked painful, and even torturous, though of course none of it went that far. Leann, like all our wonderful therapists, was highly trained and finely tuned to the needs of little baby bodies and would always stop before any exercise reached the point of serious discomfort or pain for Stephan.

After months of working with Stephan, getting him to reach and pull and move his various parts, which were ever so slowly limbering up and getting stronger, Leann stopped one day and cocked her head. "Hmm," she said as she watched Stephan half-crawl and half-"tripod" around the living room. ("Tripoding" is where a child has both hands and one knee on the floor but then props up, or tripods on the other side so that one foot is on the floor.) Leann had been taking in Stephan's every move for a while, and as she gazed at him, she seemed to come to a realization.

"Do you mind if I try something?" she asked me. Leann was a tall and lithe thirty-something woman, highly trained and tops in her field, boasting a résumé that included having been the head of pediatric physical therapy at some very elite national hospitals. I felt incredibly lucky to have her on Team Stephan.

"As long as you don't break him," I smiled. I trusted Leann, and so did Stephan; I had watched virtually every minute of every session and they had their own working relationship, with each seeming to respect the other's needs and limits, and Stephan being game as ever to always try just one more time, just stretch a little farther or bend a little more. Had Leann or any other therapist pushed him too far, Stephan wouldn't have been so trusting, but between their great skills, my constant presence, and Stephan's sheer grit and good humor, we odd bunch marched on merrily, striving for each new goal. All the many small, hard-won victories—a bent knee here, a loosened-up hip joint there, increasing recognition of words and objects—began to turn into large changes and real progress.

Leann muttered to herself as she bent down and gently turned Stephan's right ankle at the floor, adjusting it just a tiny bit, which caused him to drop gently down to all fours on the floor. He clearly did not like being in that position—it forced him to flex his hips, which were still mostly stiff and immovable, and to support himself on the strength of his arms and his core, neither of which were especially strong. Being on all fours was much harder work than his crooked tripoding.

"Aha! Do you see that?" she wowed, looking back at me. "See how that little tweak made him get on all fours?" I certainly did, though it seemed kind of amazing that one tiny move could cause Stephan to readjust his whole body position.

Leann followed Stephan around the living room for a while, gently tweaking his foot each time he propped up into the tripod position. Each time she gently turned his foot to a straighter position, Stephan adjusted downwards onto all fours, onto his hands and knees.

It was clearly hard physical work, and Stephan was being asked to discover and engage muscles that had only ever lain dormant.

After a few very up-and-down minutes, Stephan stopped, turned around, and gave Leann a grimace, as if to say, "Why me?" Leann laughed, "OK, that's enough for one day," and picked Stephan up, swinging him in an arc in front of her that made him giggle.

Leann wrapped up her session with some fun Elmo time and then set off on her way to her next appointment, her amazing skills keeping her in high demand.

In the coming weeks and months, I spent countless hours crawling around behind Stephan, turning his foot just so and getting him to drop to all fours and engage his newly discovered muscles. And bit by bit, Stephan got stronger and more confident, and eventually started to make motions towards standing up.

Summer Blackout

SUMMER IN BROOKLYN, and all of New York City, was like nothing I'd ever experienced in California. The heat was so intense, and often the air so still, that it could feel suffocating. The type of unrelenting heat where, if you showered and went outside, you would be wet with sweat in the first ninety seconds.

I remember the first time I was crossing a street, the wavy heat waves rising up from the blacktop like a mirage in an old desert adventure movie, the hero gazing hopelessly out across a vast horizon of sand, and I felt something soft and squishy underfoot. I looked down and the blacktop was actually melting. I saw a penny, heads-up for good luck, and went to pick it up but it was melted into and actually embedded in the blacktop! I looked around, incredulous, to see if any of the other passersby were as astonished as I was—the blacktop was actually *melting!*—but everyone just swerved around me, irritated expressions on their faces, and went on about their unflappable New York City–dweller ways.

That was summer heat in New York City.

One day, in the heart of Stephan's first summer, our window air conditioner units were whirring along, one upstairs and two downstairs, including a small one in Stephan's bedroom window, keeping our sweet little house cozy and cool, when the units suddenly went off and then on again. Same with the small radio that was playing in the kitchen.

Mom, who was in the midst of her three-month Brooklyn stay (and more welcome than ever as David was still usually out of town on business, as he was during this stint), looked up from where she was sitting at the table across from Stephan in his highchair, an "uh-oh" expression on her face. I paused from where I was cooking in the kitchen and held my breath until the whir of the A.C. units started up again.

"Oh my God, can you imagine if these A.C. units went off?" I said. "I think we'd all melt to death." Although, having lived in New York for some five-plus years by then, I was more accustomed to the brutal heat and humidity than was my mom.

"If those things go off, I am on the next plane back to cool California!" my mom laughed.

That afternoon, during the peak of the day's heat, Stephan was taking a nap upstairs when there was a "clunk" from somewhere and then everything went silent. Radio off, A.C. units off, no sound at all. Mom and I looked at each other.

"Uh-oh."

I opened the front door and looked out across our front porch, glancing up and down our street. Other people were doing the same, poking their heads out of their houses to see if it was just them or if everyone's power had gone out.

"Crap," I muttered, Mom gazing over my shoulder.

It was our first city-wide blackout.

As the minutes stretched to an hour, our house quickly began to heat up. It didn't take long for Stephan to start cooking away as his upstairs bedroom became still and sweltering, and he woke up from his nap sweaty and cranky.

Like so many other folks from our neighborhood, we headed out to the local hardware store in search of a battery-operated fan. Little did I know that the line at the store was already more than two hours long!

But as the afternoon stretched into evening, something magical began to happen all over our neighborhood. In the way that natural disasters can—and to be clear, a blackout in a largely well-appointed city is not actually a "disaster" but more of a huge inconvenience that would need to stretch on for a while to rate "disaster" scale—it started to bring people together.

Neighbors came out with extra flashlights to give to other neighbors, people pulled out fresh-cooked food from their refrigerators to share before it spoiled. A cluster of kids down the street enjoyed a whole box of popsicles that were rapidly melting. There were people meeting and exclaiming and sharing food on the stoops all up and down our street and on every surrounding street. And in the busiest intersection in our busy neighborhood, citizens took turns directing traffic while others became self-appointed crossing guards, helping elderly folks and moms with strollers safely traverse the still-bustling streets.

As we stood there, my hand on the stroller with sweaty little Stephan peering out at the activity around him, my eyes met my mom's, and we both choked up at the beauty of what we saw all around us: the otherwise very average-looking yuppie man playing crossing guard in the middle of the intersection, beaming with joy at his temporary designation of indispensability—and everywhere, the shared joy in selflessness, the pleasure in sharing, the connecting. I have heard others talk about the incredible generosity of spirit and enlightened soulfulness that people seem to emit during times of challenging times, and in our otherwise too-busy-to-stop New York neighborhood, they were everywhere that afternoon, washing over all of us and everything around us.

That night, with the power still out, we lit candles all over the house and were fanning ourselves with magazines and bits of paper (the hardware store had quickly sold out of battery-operated fans so our wait in line had been for nought) when it was time for Stephan's bedtime.

I put him down in his crib and he rolled around uncomfortably, his little body hot and clammy. "I'm sorry, honey," I whispered, "I know it's hot." As he started to drift off to sleep, I stood over him with a magazine and gently fanned it in his direction, making the heat a little more bearable.

I couldn't help but feel like I was a handmaiden waiting on a tiny King Tut, me standing there as the minutes stretched into an hour and then two, Stephan sleeping fitfully in his sweaty crib.

And then, sometime near dawn I think—who can remember, with me standing there, shifting my weight from one foot to the other, fanning, fanning, never stop fanning—the AC units whirred back to life, the lights went on, the radio continued singing, and the music and hum and zing of life in New York City sprang back into action.

I ran downstairs where Mom—whom we had started calling Nanny as shorthand for grandma—had been rolling restlessly on the couch. "We're back, the power is back on!"

"Wha, huh?" Her hair was stuck to her forehead.

I heard Stephan stir upstairs, a half wail, half inquisitive sound.

As I ran up the stairs towards Stephan's room, I heard Nanny utter, "Too bad…" and I knew just what she meant—if only we could retain that spirit of open neighborliness all the time.

But then the morning began, the sun barely beginning to rise, I having spent the night fanning the little king in his crib, Nanny rolling sleeplessly on the couch, Stephan sleeping away, oblivious to the chaos around him.

Sue

ON THE DAYS AND NIGHTS ROLLED, with a few therapists appearing each day to continue to work on unlocking Stephan's under-stimulated mind and body.

Sue was our occupational therapist, and I was at first not sure what an occupational therapist did. "Are you going to teach him a trade, like welding?" I laughed a bit nervously on her first appointed day.

In short, according to Wikipedia, "Occupational therapists help people of all ages to improve their ability to perform tasks in their daily living and working environments." In essence, they help a person, or a child, or a baby, function physically to the best of their ability so that they can best and most independently perform their typical daily tasks. In Stephan's case, this would mean the basic things like crawling, grasping, pulling to a stand, and gaining muscle coordination and strength.

Sue lived a few blocks away in our same Park Slope neighborhood and got around town on a scooter—not a motor scooter, but a push-with-your-feet-like-a-little-kid scooter. And Sue was indeed the best possible combination of extremely well-trained professional (these therapists require master's degrees, like most of the others, and their training is also medical in nature) with the joyous enthusiasm of a child.

Sue was then probably in her forties, with a happy grin and easy laugh and a very natural, whip-smart, Earth Mother vibe. Sue had two college-aged sons and a husband who was battling colon cancer. (Tragically, he later lost that battle.) Sue and her husband had been instrumental in raising funds for Significant Steps, what was then a beautiful and newly built early childhood development facility in Park Slope, which unfortunately later went bankrupt.

Sue started slowly and gently testing Stephan's flexibility and strength, both of which were minimal. She had a long canvas "tunnel" that folded up like an accordion (physical therapist Leann had the same toy) and would put a stuffed Elmo doll or a small car inside that would necessitate Stephan's getting down on all fours to crawl through to retrieve.

Sue seemed to hone in on Stephan's hips and how stiff they were. She did some of the same things as Leann, but Sue seemed to get down deeper into Stephan's little muscles, as if she were trying to loosen a long-rusted hinge.

Sue would often sit near Stephan on the floor and hold an object he desired near his shoulder so that he would have to reach across his body for it, turning his torso completely sideways and stretching his shoulders and torso and hips. Or she would hold something just in front of or behind him and when he went to reach for it, she would gently hold his hips and bottom to the floor so that he had to do the stretching specifically from his stiff hips. Stephan never actually grunted but you could tell how hard it was for him to stretch and move and reach.

To his eternal credit, Stephan never once turned away or gave up or refused to reach for something when prompted. He kept at it, day after day and week after week, even when he got big enough to go to the facilities at Significant Steps, where Sue would have him step through tires on the ground, climb up a rope ladder, or swing from a tire swing, all "play" activities that engaged his little body and helped unstick his rusty joints.

"I'm trying to open them up," Sue would say when she sometimes ended a very challenging session with a baby massage near Stephan's hard-working hip joints. Sue was good at pushing Stephan a bit further and a bit further, but she was great at reading him and would always stop just before Stephan hit the burnout stage, often when he was beginning to turn a look of consternation her way.

"Okay, okay, great job, that's enough for now," she would smile, and ease her touch from a prodding, deep-muscle challenge into a calming, comforting massage. Sue showed me key areas to massage, as well as those to avoid, and after a rough day or during a sleepless night, I would often rub Stephan's feet or back or head—his favorite was and is still a scalp massage—and watch while his hard-working limbs and muscles relaxed.

My friend Sylvia, an early childhood development expert who runs a preschool, said, "You know, you probably re-wired Stephan's brain with all that one-on-one intervention," and I imagine that she may be right. Stephan, and likely most babies, seemed equally resilient and helpless, and since I was there for virtually every minute of every session, the changes Stephan was making moment to moment seemed gradual. But looking back I can see that he really was making huge, amazing strides on pretty much a daily and weekly basis. Maybe the biggest stride of all was that Stephan was getting accustomed to and even comfortable with sitting down and *focusing* whenever a teacher or someone he respected sat across from him (though he did not suffer fools, and he did not love or respond to every speech therapist; more on that later).

Still, just when I thought we had settled into a reliable groove—therapy in the morning, a snack and walk, nap, lunch, more therapy, dinner, bath, reading, bedtime—suddenly I found us in a new chapter.

Night Terrors

STEPHAN HAD BECOME a decent sleeper once he realized that he was in his forever home and that when he cried, I always appeared. With all his basic needs met—and then some—he seemed mostly content.

And then came the night terrors.

The first time it happened, Stephan had been asleep for a few hours and I was relaxing in another room with a glass of wine when suddenly, seemingly out of nowhere, he screamed louder and with more desperation than I had ever heard. I literally went running up the stairs two at a time to see if he had gotten his foot or arm stuck in his crib or something wrapped around his neck. I flung open the door and there he was, standing up in his crib, hanging onto the side, his eyes in a wide-open stare, shrieking at the top of his lungs.

"Honey, honey," I murmured as I went to his side. But Stephan looked right past me like I wasn't there. I picked him up but he was squirming and resisting and it was like trying to hold an angry, hyper-greased octopus, so I put him back down in his bed. His screaming hadn't subsided at all and my ears were still ringing from having had his head right next to mine.

I instinctively tried to keep him from thrashing around, but luckily he was too little to get much physical momentum going. I touched and caressed him every now and then but it seemed to have no effect. Eventually he quieted down and let me tuck him back in and he went right back to sleep. I, of course, lay awake the rest of the night listening in case he stirred again.

Who knew what was going through his baby mind during those moments? I couldn't help but think that it was related to all the stress and anguish of his exceptional young life to that point; maybe it sprang from a primeval sense of abandonment or loneliness or anger. But then again, maybe it wasn't that at all—maybe Stephan would have had exactly the same experience if he had had a "perfect" and healthy start in life.

I would never know for sure.

Stephan's night terrors continued more or less nightly, sometimes more than once a night, for a few months, and I began to understand how the myth of demonic children might have evolved from babies with night terrors.

During that sleepless and stressful chapter, I tried to remember what my friend Nina had said when I had queried my parent friends as to their single best piece of advice about parenting: "Everything is a phase."

And to this day, that rings so true. Whether it is teething or night terrors or potty training—or dealing with a surly teenager— that thing that is either wonderful or driving you batty will suddenly whoosh away and disappear out of your life and a brand-new thing, wonderful or awful, will leap into its place. I think the key is to remember that everything is temporary and enjoy *all* of the moments, especially all the daily milestones that seem to flash by like signs on a desert highway, a colorful whoosh and blur and suddenly it is behind you. You turn and crane your neck to try to get a clearer view but it is already long gone and fading into the past.

Fever

SOMETIME DURING STEPHAN'S first Brooklyn summer, after the blackout and before the summer swelter cooled to the crisp of fall, Stephan got his first big, bad infection.

For the most part, and despite his shaky debut on the planet in terms of health, Stephan had motored along fairly consistently since he got home in May. Some sniffles and colds here and there, but no chronic ear infections that so many kids get, nothing horrible that we couldn't shake with over-the-counter medicines.

And then he got a cough that wouldn't go away with the usual treatment, and then he quickly spiked a fever. It was 100, then 101 degrees. I called our doctor, whose office was a half-mile or so away. By the time the nurse got on the phone, Stephan's fever was 102.

As I told the nurse how much Tylenol I had given Stephan—just the usual dose thus far—my mom was filling the tub with cold water. The nurse suggested we give it a few minutes and see if the Tylenol would start to bring the fever down, and agreed that a cold bath might help.

By this time it was getting late in the afternoon and I was keeping my eye on the clock knowing that the doctor's office closed at six P.M.

Stephan wailed when I gently dipped him in the cold water— who could blame him?—and I very softly splashed the water on him, working my way up to his torso. Thank goodness Nanny was there to offer support and a calming "been there, done that" demeanor.

A few minutes later as I toweled off Stephan's tiny steaming body, I could feel that he had not cooled off much. I loosely bundled him up in the damp towel and walked around the house with him, singing a little song, trying to get him more comfortable. He squirmed and whined, which he rarely did.

Thirty minutes later his temperature had risen to 103. I called the doctor again and had trouble getting through to a live person (even back then, Park Slope was swarming with young families, and there was often a two-hour wait at the doctor's office). My throat was beginning to tighten, and despite my mom's assurances that he would be fine and to just keep doing what we were doing, I couldn't help but remember how wan and tiny Stephan had been back in the orphanage, how he'd weighed only two pounds at birth, how hard he had had to fight to simply survive. He had never been and still was not a typically robust American-born baby who could fight off nasty germs with one good nap and then wake up laughing. Stephan's health was and had always to that point been delicate, and despite Nanny's typically Russian loving but stern demeanor of "buck up, you'll be fine," I was increasingly worried that Stephan might not be fine.

I stopped pacing and looked at the clock yet again. It was after five. I got Stephan dressed and took my time fanning him off when he was just in a diaper. I took his temperature again. 103.5. I called the doctor's office again but couldn't reach a live person. I fanned Stephan some more, tried to get him to drink some cool juice—he wouldn't—took his temperature again. 104!

That's it! I thought, I'm outta here! It was by that time 5:45, so I had fifteen minutes to get to the doctor's office. I wasn't going to bother to try to call them again, or to call a cab, I was just going to literally run over there.

I threw on my shoes. "Mom, either wait here or follow me," I shouted over my shoulder, Stephan in my arms as I flung open the front door. I ran out without bothering with the stroller.

"Wait, wait," Mom shouted as I bolted down the street, Stephan under my right arm like an unwieldy, hot pink football.

I ran up our block, over two blocks, up one more double-long block, and then down about three more, waving my one free arm to stop traffic as I crossed intersections, my face apparently bearing an expression that made cars yield to me. I could not feel my body, I was not panting, I didn't feel winded—I was just in a blind panic to get Stephan's fever down and that was the one and only thing that propelled me down the street.

Stephan was mainly quiet, jostling along under my arm, Mom trailing a block or so behind me but gamely still there.

Finally, I got to the building where the doctor's office was. I punched the elevator button. It was 6:01.

When the elevator door opened, the nurses were starting to close the office. "Wait, wait," I yelled as I ran through the lobby and straight through the doors towards the exam rooms. "I called a bunch of times earlier, my son Stephan has a terrible fever..." The nurses did not try to stop me.

The doctor came in—Stephan's temperature was still 104. The doctor gave Stephan a mega-dose of Tylenol to try to jump-start his fever in reverse, the liquid kind that you take orally via a large syringe. Mom had just arrived as well and leaned panting against the door.

But my little Boo—a few seconds after he had gotten the mega-dose of medicine and we had all just stopped to catch our breaths—from my cradled arms Stephan emitted an impossibly huge projectile vomit, so amazingly robust that it formed a perfect rainbow shape of bright-pink liquid Tylenol that shot three feet up in the air and all the way across the room, until it finally landed directly on the front of the doctor's white coat.

I just stood there, slack-jawed. "I didn't know that was even possible..." I stammered. I thought of making a joke about a pot of gold at the end of the Tylenol rainbow but thought better of it.

The doctor smiled, seemingly unfazed. "I think that enough of it stayed down there that it should help him," he said.

We stood around for a few minutes until they took Stephan's temperature again. It had gone down to 103. Phew! The doctor let us hang around for a few more minutes—Stephan's temperature was by then 102.5—and assured me that I could reach him any time day or night if things got worse, but he felt confident that Stephan's fever had broken and that we would slowly get back to normal.

Mom and Stephan and I made our way slowly back home, a bedraggled but relieved little bunch. Stephan seemed so heavy in my arms on the way back now that I could feel my body again!

When we got home, Stephan finally wanted to stay in his crib and drifted into a deep sleep, while Mom and I opened a bottle of wine. "Phew!" I said, "I can finally exhale."

Mom and I chatted for a bit until she felt comfortable leaving Stephan and me and going back to her little sublet. Thank goodness she was there, I thought for the umpteenth time as I flopped down onto my bed in a state of utter exhaustion.

Sandra

AND ON THE EARLY INTERVENTION went, our days and lives entirely folded around Stephan's needs and therapies.

We had been lucky—and I had been insistent—on getting great therapists to work with Stephan. Tasia in special ed was amazing, a real life-changer. Same was true for Sue in occupational and Leann in physical therapy. When it came to speech therapy, however, it proved to be a bit tougher.

The first young woman we had was okay; Lauren seemed to have the basic skills and training but lacked the passion of the rest of Stephan's therapists, and he could tell. With her bright-red hair and pale skin, she spent lots of time telling me about gardening in her bathing suit out on Long Island trying to get tan before her wedding. She went through the motions but her heart wasn't in it, so eventually we replaced her. After that we had another mediocre person, I can't remember her name, who also showed up and did cursory exercises but didn't really connect with Stephan.

Happily, Stephan had grown accustomed to having amazing, impassioned therapist/teachers sit nose to nose with him every day and pour their wits and love and humor into each session, so when someone showed up with anything less than that, he could tell the difference. There were times when Stephan actually glanced over at me during a mediocre session as if to say, *"Really?* This is how we're going to spend my precious time?" Still, by about two years old

Stephan could say "truck" (though only I could actually understand it) and was trying to say some other words like "mama" and "car" (of course). His diction was super-muddy, but I figured it was the norm for his age given his background.

The second—or third—run-of-the-mill speech therapist was asked via the agency not to come back. "I just don't think we've found the right fit yet," I explained over the phone. Luckily, early intervention services were free in New York City at that point—I don't know how things are today—but you still had to be a fierce advocate on behalf of your child, the proverbial squeaky wheel. And Stephan on paper looked extremely needy, so they weren't likely to give me a hard time in terms of services. Still, they were not pleased with my too-frequent calls regarding speech therapy.

"Can we get just one more referral? Really, my son works so hard, I know if we find the right person it will shorten the amount of time he requires services." Bingo—I had said the magic words.

"Okay," the woman said reluctantly.

And that's when Sasa showed up.

Sandra was her real name—Sasa was Stephan's name for her—and the first thing you noticed about her was that she was a total knockout physically. She was distractingly beautiful, with long, thick black hair, olive skin, and aquiline features. And she had a figure that snapped men's heads around when she walked by. None of this was relevant to the amazing work she did of course but it was funny to notice my tiny little Stephan noticing her—he was smitten with her and he was barely a toddler!

Sandra loved her job and it showed. She would come in and get right to work; she'd pull out a foot-high plastic toy garage full of cars, an Elmo doll, books with words that you had to point to. She spoke very deliberately and slowly to get Stephan to try harder to repeat words, something he had always been reluctant to do, and she was direct to just this side of obnoxious, which Stephan seemed to appreciate (no wilting flowers for this boy!). It was and had always been clear that Stephan understood what words meant, and he would unfailingly point to the correct picture of things when their corresponding names were spoken. He just couldn't say the words himself.

Sandra worked with Stephan for a few months and was making real progress with him. Stephan was always happy to see her, and he always tried his best to do what she asked of him. Sandra challenged Stephan; she would pull out a page with twenty pictures on it and say, "Dog. Stephan, show me the dog." Stephan could always correctly identify the picture on the page but would say something undecipherable, like "mwah." Sandra would say, "Car, show me the car," and Stephan would point to the picture of the car and again say "mwah." He couldn't seem to enunciate an actual sound or word but he clearly knew the names and could identify the different objects.

I could see that Sandra was mulling something over in her mind, trying to connect the dots between Stephan's clearly very bright and curious intellect and his confounding lack of intelligible sounds or speech.

And then one day, Sandra came in, sat down, and said, "I think Stephan has verbal apraxia." She explained to me that verbal apraxia was, in essence, where the brain knew what it wanted to say but couldn't successfully transmit the signal to the mouth and mouth muscles to get the words out. And that could be accounting as well for Stephan's reluctance to try out new words and sounds.

Oh my God, I thought, *that makes perfect sense!*

Once Sandra told me what it was, it seemed so obvious that it was a relief. Not that I had lost sleep specifically over Stephan's speech or lack of same—the truth is, I was way too busy with the whole she-bang, the physical, occupational, special ed and speech therapies, not to mention night terrors and functioning like a single mom given David's constant work travel scedule.

Shortly thereafter, at Sandra's suggestion, we began prompt training, where you literally help form and squeeze and shape the child's mouth into the shape like "o" or "e" needed to say a word. We used popsicle sticks, lollipops, any and everything to get Stephan's muscles to wake up and connect to his brain.

After some weeks of prompt training—which Stephan did not

enjoy (who wants someone sticking something into your mouth when you're being asked to speak?)—we started to realize that Stephan could say vertical sounds like "ah" or "mah" but was having much more trouble with horizontal sounds like "ee" or "me." And that realization led us to a whole new series of goals and challenges for the coming weeks and months.

Thank goodness for our Sasa! Sandra was utterly crucial in helping to unlock Stephan's speech. In fact, largely inspired by the brilliant and beautiful Sandra, some years later I actually went back to school to pursue a degree in pediatric speech therapy. But divorce and finances and the reality of single-parenthood intervened and I didn't have the luxury of just going to school, so I opted to go back into the entertainment industry that I knew so well.

But I will never forget Sandra, our Sasa—it was her passion for her work and her unending drive for answers that helped unlock the world of speech for Stephan, and for that I will be forever grateful.

A Real Mother

IT WAS NEVER A SERIOUS PART of my desire to become a parent that a child should look like me physically. Of course, there were moments mid-IVF treatment where 100 percent of my being, mental and physical, was solely obsessed with whether our two little chromosomes, seed and sperm, would successfully come together to make a new One, and that One would surely have some resemblance to the two parts from which it sprang. My family is known for blue eyes, something I did think of and wonder whether a child would inherit during that painful chapter. But even then, it wasn't a driving force or a goal I yearned for, but more a passing thought à la "wouldn't it be cool if…" The baby boy whom we got closest to adopting during the debacle in Rochester in upstate New York had an African American/Japanese Birth Father and an Italian American Birth Mother and was a beautiful infant who likely has grown up to be a good-looking young man.

I find diversity to be among the most inspiring aspects of our humanity, a kind of tangible gorgeous tapestry reflecting the world in which we live, and love the fact that people travel to and from all parts of the world and fall in love with and often make children with other folks from different parts of the world. Having a child that looked like me was never something that was a goal in my heart or mind.

And so it was a surprise and very ironic that Stephan has turned out to look very much like me, like my brother his uncle, and in general like our partly Russian-bred family. As I said earlier, adopting a child from Russia was never a goal despite my having maternal Russian roots of which I am very proud. With similar blondish hair and fair skin, and with the same hazel/amber eyes as my Russian-born grandmother who had immigrated from Belarus (then part of the Soviet Union) to the United States as a young girl, Stephan looks born and plucked from the same tree as me. As us. When he would walk down the street with his uncle, my tall, goofy older brother with a mane of surf-blond hair, Stephan looked like his mini-me, and something about that felt good and made me laugh, and I could see that Stephan got a kick out of people saying, "Wow, that kid looks just like you!" to my brother.

When I used to fly back to Los Angeles from Brooklyn when Stephan was a toddler, he was always so well behaved—no more constant screaming on planes for this boy—that folks would *ooh* and *aah* over him, Stephan with his golden curls and hushed demeanor (maybe everyone loves a cute and silent baby on a plane). I remember one trip where a stewardess was smitten with my little Stephan, and she cooed over him every time she passed our seat. When we landed, she even had the pilot open the cockpit door so Stephan could take a peek inside and say hello to the pilot. As we were disembarking, the stewardess said as she gestured at Stephan, "He's wonderful, you should make some more of those." If only you knew, I thought, but simply smiled and said thanks.

On a deeper level, there have been times when in a very basic, animal way, I think our looking similar has been a comfort to Stephan. On first days of school, for example, especially when he was young and still very shy, Stephan seemed to take comfort in looking like he was part of a larger family group, to blend in and not draw any attention to himself or inspire looks or questions. To see our family all together, Nanny and me and my sister and brother and Stephan, Stephan looks exactly like the rest of us, and I have seen him respond happily when people have remarked on it over the years. Perhaps it is an animal instinct, that drive to look like you belong to the herd with whom you roam.

I have always lived in neighborhoods that were full of socio-economic and racial diversity—at least when I got there if not when I left—whether it was in Brooklyn or L.A., where Stephan's public schools were and are very diverse, with kids from a wide array of racial, ethnic, and socioeconomic backgrounds. I believe that the constant diversity of Stephan's surroundings has been one of the reasons that he has grown up seeing all kinds of different folks as equal in terms of their value and contribution. Because he has lived it and knows it to be true.

But still the animal part of us humans makes certain assumptions, sometimes based on physical attributes, sometimes based on presumed social or familial connections, and that goes for the idea of adoption versus a baby being birthed from one's loins as well.

Case in point: I remember once sitting in the waiting room of the local hospital in Brooklyn when Stephan was around two years old. I started talking with a fellow mother also holding her baby. She wore a beautiful batiked headscarf and had the gorgeous lilting accent of one of the West African countries. After a few minutes she commented that Stephan looked just like me. "Funny, isn't it," I smiled, "especially since he is actually adopted."

She looked at me with surprise. "Oh, so you're not his real mother."

I think my mouth hung open for a minute. We were at that moment sitting and waiting in the hospital due to an ongoing bout of fever that had kept Stephan and me awake every night for more than a week. What did she mean, not his "real" mother? I had shepherded him home, to his real and forever home, from a faraway land. I had been wiping up his poo and collecting it in specimen bags for months. I was present for every single early intervention session he had, was with him twenty-four hours a day, comforted him when he was scared, was ushering him into the world of food and books and baths, and most of all, loved him insanely, every ounce of his tiny being. I would die for him. You could not convince me that he and I were not meant to find each other. Suffice to say, I could not be any more his "real mother."

I was affronted by her suggestion, albeit one based on ignorance, though as a fellow mother, I thought she would well know the reality of what parenting really is, with the nine months it takes to cook up a baby a mere precursor to the lifetime of constant needs that follows.

I considered launching into this explanation but then a nurse called the woman and her baby away to the exam room and she stood up and disappeared down the hallway.

Anniversaries

MARCH 21 MARKS THE ANNIVERSARY of the day I met Stephan
in Russia in 2003.

When you have an adopted child, there are a number of anni-
versaries you celebrate: the day you met your child; the day your
child became officially, legally yours; the day you brought your child
home (if it is different); and lastly, your child's actual birthday. For
me, the most emotional of them is often this one, March 21, the day
I first met Stephan; the image of him being brought through the
big blue-and-white doors of the orphanage, bundled up like a tiny,
overheated burlap sack, the *babushka* cradling him and grinning at
me, my instinctive comment that "He's alive…" when I first laid eyes
on him and saw his alarmed and depressed but very alive expression,
especially after meeting so many permanently sick babies in Siberia.

March 21, 2003, which happened to also be the first day of
spring, is one that I will remember forever.

I will remember the date—that year, that week, that day and the
precise moment—forever, since it was a day that so indelibly changed
both my and Stephan's lives. The impact it has had and continues
to have on us; how my heart swelled when I saw him, the weight of
all of the preceding years, of lost pregnancies and ridiculously failed
domestic adoptions, the in vitro and cost and pain and needles and
moods and absurdity of the whole proposition. Stephan's amazing,
heartbreaking grit and determination, how such a tiny little being

survived and then thrived against all odds, and how improbable that we found each other literally on opposite sides of the planet—it still chokes me up when I think about it.

On Stephan's actual birthday, August 9, I can't help but think, "This should have been October 9" or something close to it. What if Stephan had been full term? Would he have faced—and continue to face—the challenges that have sometimes dogged him? But I will never know. Birthdays are a sacred fun day in our family and we try to celebrate the heck out of them every year.

And I have to admit, I have come to a mostly peaceful place with the what-ifs—what if Stephan had been full term? What if he'd had decent food in the orphanage? What if he'd been held or spoken to, or allowed to crawl?

But I also remind myself that I know plenty of people who had been absolutely healthy when they gave birth to their children, and those kids had sometimes turned out to have serious, permanent issues, many of them even more daunting than Stephan's. The fact is, once you sign on to being a parent, whether purposely (and sometimes later in life) like me, or often more unwittingly, when younger and more prone to an "oops!" moment, parenting is a total crap shoot and is permanent.

I remember when I was on the motherhood quest and in constant yearning and emotional anguish, often watching young mothers yank around their kids on New York subways and thinking, "You need a license to get a dog or catch a fish—why not to have a child?"

But once you are a parent, all the what-ifs go out the window, as does everything else. You are on the train, it has left the station, and all you can do is hang on and try to do your best in what often seem crazy, ridiculous, impossible, and exhausting situations.

And so on our lives went, me and Stephan, all the history that had led up to that point truly out of my mind on a daily basis. I was consumed with the tasks at hand, which took every waking moment of mental and physical energy (and plenty that should have been sleeping ones as well), which was really no different from any parent of a young child.

After months of angsting over it, I decided I simply could not bear to go back to full-time work, and to finally make that definite decision was a big relief. Shortly thereafter, I started a consulting company doing the same kind of music marketing I had been doing, and that allowed me to work a few days a week as clients needed, add a twice-weekly babysitter into the mix, and bring in some money.

The days turned into weeks, the therapies continued, and Stephan remained an unbelievable trooper and faced every challenge head on. His golden curls turned a hue darker and started to straighten just a little (I was so sad to see them fade!), and bit by bit he continued to grow and gain strength as the seasons kept rolling from summer to fall to winter to spring and back again to summer.

It was a blissful time and I am so grateful to have had the ability to concentrate on Stephan's every need in what were irreplaceably beautiful and vital days.

To Run or Not to Run

STEPHAN'S EARLY INTERVENTION therapies continued; Sandra had Stephan starting to enunciate horizontally as well as vertically and all the vowel sounds were starting to come out; Tasia continued her magic and I'm sure laid the foundation for Stephan to trust teachers and enjoy the wonder of discovery; Leann had me running with Stephan in Prospect Park (or more aptly, I spent hours running back and forth, waving my arms trying to get him to either run towards me, run after me, or run in general, something he was never that crazy about doing); and Sue continued to delight in Stephan's growth and learning while always challenging him to stretch a little farther or bend a little more while continuing to massage his stiff little hips, the loosening of which she seemed to have taken on as her personal mission.

Slowly and very arduously, and with me always just one step behind him, little Stephan started to grow and learn and gain strength, and eventually began to, if not master, then at least be capable of expressing himself in every area. He could talk, he could walk and run, he could bend and grasp and reach for things and go to a toddler party and not look out of place amongst other "normal" kids.

It bears repeating—never once did Stephan ever turn away from or refuse to participate in a single one of the hundreds of hours of lessons and therapy sessions he received. There was speech therapy, me pushing and prodding his cheeks and lips and tongue into the respective shapes his mouth was struggling to form; Stephan being challenged to twist his stiff body in ways that were uncomfortable, at the least, as he crawled through tunnels and grasped for toys just out of reach; endless hours of being asked to focus, to try one more time, always to push just a little further and try just a little harder.

One at a time, each individual therapist came to me on her own after a year or two of working with him and after Stephan had surpassed her expectations; each one told me with good humor and a conspiratorial wink that they hadn't wanted to tell me when we had first started, but they had never expected Stephan to be able to master the respective skill she had been sharing with him (the exception being Tasia, who had witnessed the Chicken Moment and been a true believer ever since). Whether it was speech, delicate and/or strength-oriented fine motor skills, or strenuous physical activities, each therapist marveled at Stephan's fierce determination and how he had overcome their previous dire predictions about his future capabilities.

"Hah, I love it, never say never and never give up, that's my boy!" I laughed.

During one especially laborious session in Prospect Park, somehow two-year-old, angelic-looking Stephan had Leann and me running around like crazed chickens while he mostly stood around grinning. It was not until the session was over, Leann and I both exhausted from exerting so much energy trying to entice Stephan to run as fast as he could, to challenge his balance and muscles, to run either towards us or away from us, any which way really, and finally, once we stopped, panting and sweating, Stephan—finally—merrily took off at a fast clip in the opposite direction, that Leann turned to me and confessed, "You know, I didn't want to say this when we first started a year or two ago, but I never thought Stephan would be able to walk, much less run."

While we both stood there, sweating, slack-jawed, watching Stephan gleefully weave and wobble his way across a large grassy field, Leann marveled, "Man, he's fast when he wants to be." The air was still for a beat, then we slowly looked towards each other; Leann's usually perfect hair was stuck to her damp forehead and her shirt was askew, I was grass-stained and dripping sweat. We looked back towards Stephan, who was giggling like mad, obviously getting a kick out of having exercised total control over us.

I looked back at Leann and we both understood the hilarity of what had happened, of this tiny little boo-boo toddler having moved us around like chess pieces for forty-five minutes and then run off in celebration of his accomplishment.

Stephan was out in the middle of the beautiful green field, a two-foot-high king, grinning from ear to ear. "Maaaaaa!" he screeched happily in my direction.

Leann and I looked at him for a beat, then burst out laughing, enjoying the absurdity of it all, and I took off in a happy jog to go scoop up my marvelous and amazing boy.

Once I gathered up Stephan and said goodbye to Leann, we strolled back towards our house and I thought of Leann's comment—"I never thought he would walk, much less run"—and marveled again at how fortunate it had been, my and Stephan's original level of blissful ignorance. Had either one of us known what lay ahead in each hour of therapy—the dire assessments leading to very serious challenges, the endless hours of work, the mounds of paperwork and my nightly phone calls insisting that my son still needed the therapy, thank you—we might have stalled before we had really begun.

The weight of the knowledge would not have prevented me from pursuing the therapies Stephan needed—once his grim diagnoses were clear, wild horses couldn't have kept me from securing the very best help available—but the weight of the knowledge, of what it could really mean, could have been exhausting and might have cast a shadow on our actions, as if Stephan were doomed to being "less than" unless proven otherwise.

As it was, when I looked at Stephan, nothing else consciously mattered. All I saw was the culmination of a dream and sheer, beautiful possibility—not the years of lost pregnancies and IVF, not the crazy domestic adoption debacles, not Stephan's terrible start in life and first sickly, hospitalized, underfed nine months on the planet; what I saw when I looked at Stephan was hope. Love. A gleaming promise of something bright and sweet. He was so smart! He was so beautiful! He was so willing to work his tiny baby mind and body off to get to the next step, never mind what step might come after that.

It was literally one step in front of the other, and thankfully Stephan and I were a matched pair in thinking that each individual step was glorious in itself, and celebrated each day's tiny victories, never focusing on what would follow.

Memories and Milestones

WHEN STEPHAN WAS ABOUT two and a half years old, Tasia recommended that he would benefit from going to a play school to interact with other kids and teachers and said there was a wonderful one not far from our house. So, I enrolled Stephan and toted him off on the first day, then slowly died inside as he wailed and screeched and reached his desperate little pink hand out towards me when I went to leave.

Slowly Stephan grew more accustomed to the school setting and even when our favorite teacher left, we stayed for the remainder of the baby school year, the class using the basement with the furnace as the playground during winter storms and playing on the small cement yard during good weather.

We spent Stephan's third birthday in Normandy, France staying with Nanny and my sister at a lovely home that belonged to some friends of friends of my mother's. On a day trip to the town of Rouen, I paid some Gypsies to sing "Happy Birthday" to Stephan on August 9, while we sat in an outdoor café steps from the wall where Joan of Arc had been burned (I only discovered when we got back home to New York that Stephan had pulled a good-size chunk from the wall and stuffed it in his pocket). France is where Stephan learned to love croissants, which remain his favorite treat today.

I had long known that something was amiss in my relationship with David—we had been in therapy with no changes in sight for many years by this point, but how could one have a real or healthy relationship with someone who was usually absent?—and it became acutely obvious during our France trip, during which David's emotional state fluctuated between cranky and distant.

At the end of the year, after David's longtime job had ended, after he had spent a brief and tumultuous time at a new job during which he frequently worked late into the night, his then-boss arranged for him to get yet another newer job in Los Angeles. This was perfect in my mind as I was suddenly done with the winter weather—have you tried pushing a stroller though mounds of gray frozen snow and icy puddles?—and so we moved back to Los Angeles.

I was relieved to be closer to my family, and once we were settled in, Stephan started preschool (and sobbed nonstop while singing Christmas songs during his preschool holiday recital). I had always kept an eye on Stephan's progress, emotionally and academically, and welcomed his teachers' insights into what they thought was in his best interest. When Stephan was about to graduate from preschool, his teacher, a wonderful and gifted woman with a calm and loving demeanor, said, "I think he's ready; there's no reason to hold back another year." And she was right; Stephan was and remains a child who likes "scaffolding," reaching up and forward in a learning environment and being challenged rather than being overly comfortable and complacent.

It was shortly after our move to L.A. and during Stephan's preschool years that I got divorced from David (exactly what lead to it is a whole other story); although it was of course very difficult, it was a bit less so than it might have been since David had been largely absent for so much of his young life that Stephan's day-to-day reality did not drastically change.

Admittedly I had long known something was amiss in my marriage, but I had been so single-minded about becoming a mother that everything else, including my own relationship, had been shoved to the back burner. I knew in my gut that this aspect of my life would eventually come to the fore and need to be faced, but at first I was too much on the parenthood quest, and then later I was too busy being a kid-drunk, new-baby mom to turn towards it. But then there it suddenly was.

I made sure to shield and inform Stephan as much as I could in an age-appropriate way (I think he was four years old at the time) and told him that we as adults had decided that we would be better parents and better friends if we didn't live together, but that we would always be Stephan's parents—I would always be his mom and David would always be his dad. And that this change had nothing to do with Stephan, it was between us adults—"Sometimes grownups agree to disagree," I told him.

One of the hardest things I have ever done was to stay positive about his dad in front of Stephan; it would do no one any good for me to sound bitter about his father, and even though I was angry as hell, sad, and disappointed about the divorce, in my gut I had known it was coming and my sole focus became on keeping Stephan as healthy as possible during a difficult time.

Despite his going through financial hardship and bouncing around to different houses during the post-divorce years, I made sure that, once I knew that David and the company he was keeping were appropriate for a young child to be around, he could continue to be a part of Stephan's life. Any and all aspects of our day-to day-reality and life always were and remain solely on me, from school meetings to birthday parties to doctor's appointments.

Still, life marched on and Stephan made it grudgingly through kindergarten—he had been lucky to get accustomed to having passionate and gifted teachers in early intervention and preschool, and when faced with someone merely adequate he was very nonplussed. But as we all did, Stephan weathered some not-so-great teachers and enjoyed some amazing ones (some teachers thought he had lingering learning issues, some thought he was gifted, which points out how vital active parenting is, since one seems to have to constantly advocate for one's child). Luckily, I was able to land Stephan in a wonderful, kindhearted, and progressive charter elementary school where we met Mr. Jason Latif Bozé, aka Mr. Bozé, a tall, gentle man and teacher extraordinaire whose expertise was math but whose lasting impact on Stephan's life came in the form of his really seeing and *getting* Stephan, of recognizing his particular personal skills and personality strengths and celebrating them.

Stephan entered Open Charter Magnet School in third grade and as the school year was already in progress, he stuck out as a "new kid," but luckily he seemed to feel immediately at home with Mr. Bozé, and within the very first week Stephan was sitting in the front row of his class, offering to help the teachers or run errands and happily assisting other kids at every chance he got. He was even awarded a special certificate for courage, having entered the school late in the year and jumped right in as if he'd been there forever.

That was one of my first real glimpses of the strength of character Stephan was developing as an individual, though I had seen the spark of it way back in Russia that very first day I had laid eyes on him, that innate "never say never" spirit.

Watching Stephan leap towards his own blossoming after having been fueled by this bit of respect and recognition from a grown-up, from a person of authority, I learned a valuable lesson from Mr. Bozé, and that is to expect great and special things from my child, and to celebrate his effort more than a particular result. To expect my child to succeed, whatever those details looked like for him. It's like one of those self-fulfilling prophecies, where self-doubt makes one prone to failure and self-confidence makes one prone to succeed. You know how it is when someone always tells you, for example, that you're clumsy. You will find yourself inexplicably being clumsy around them! And so we parents—as well as teachers, babysitters, grown-ups of all sorts—have this enormous, often permanent effect on our children; this is something of which I was already aware, but to see it so beautifully affect my child in a real-life, everyday way made an indelible mark on me as well as on Stephan.

It wasn't long before Stephan's leadership skills were coming to the fore and his willingness to lean towards tasks really shone through (he and a buddy were later famous in fifth grade for their upkeep of a riverbed table and the attendant fish and other wildlife they kept in the classroom). A few years later, when we were having issues with Stephan's middle school and had gone to visit Open Charter, Mr. Bozé was in disbelief—"How could they not see him, how could they not see *this*?" Mr. Bozé had pointed towards Stephan, who had stopped the game he was in the middle of to help out some younger kids, all with a big grin on his face.

Stephan continued speech therapy throughout elementary school, primarily due to a lingering lisp and some enunciation difficulty (though by fourth grade he was complaining about being pulled out of class, for which I could not blame him), and was often tested for general skills given his rough start, but proved to be a bright, capable, and happy boy, in the mainstream academically and socially (and, as it turned out, a natural leader amongst his peers).

There were field trips to museums, a camping trip to the Channel Islands—the fact that the wind blew ferociously and sent the tents flying away across a meadow in the middle of the island made the trip especially fun and memorable for Stephan and his buddies—good friends, holiday events, and an after-school rock band with which Stephan played bass guitar and got to perform at the House of Blues.

I have never been a fan of "traditional" formal education as it is in the U.S., with standardized testing being the culmination of everything I think does not work about the way we do it. "I don't care about your grades," I began telling Stephan way back in elementary school—"I care whether you did your best. Whether you did all the assignments, studied, thought critically, and hopefully got even more curious about whatever subject you're studying. If you did all of that and got a C on a test, I love that C. If you sleepwalk through a class, don't try hard and don't absorb much and still get an A, I do not like that A since it won't have much meaning or value to you."

I, the hippy-dippy, "let kids play to learn" mom—wouldn't it just figure then, that as soon as Stephan got towards the upper grades of elementary school, he showed just how driven and Type-A he naturally is; he cared and still cares deeply about grades and is extremely driven to excel. If he gets a less-than-superb score on some work he gets really ticked off. I know how lucky I am as a parent to have a child with his attitude, and it has been great to watch him soar academically; it has been equally odd to watch some parents be solely hyper-focused on grades, which seems to have the opposite of the desired effect in that many of their kids then do their darndest to get crummy grades. The old parent–child power dynamic at play…

It was during his elementary school years that Stephan seemed to suddenly, almost overnight, become a computer and tech expert. When he came home one day during fifth grade and said "Guess what Mom?—I fixed all the computers at school," I said "That's great, way to go honey!" but privately thought *Hmm, I rather doubt he seriously fixed a computer. It's not like he's ever taken a class or anything…*

But the next day when I dropped him off at school and happened to ask his teacher, she said that yes, Stephan had indeed fixed all the computers! He had apparently volunteered to help the tech officer in charge of the computer system, and once he had access to the bowels of their tech setup, Stephan had somehow rebooted and or tweaked the system so it worked properly.

"How did you know how to fix the school computers?" I asked Stephan later.

"I dunno, I just figured it out" Stephan said nonchalantly. Having grown up with computers, unlike my generation, Stephan and his peers are fearless with all things tech.

"Must be those Russian genes," I laughed. "Use your powers for good, not evil!"

It was shortly thereafter that Stephan taught himself coding to the degree that he started his own online Minecraft business, something he continues all these years later, and which has evolved into an international, money-making endeavor, and one in which he has included numerous friends. Stephan got so expert at programming and fixing computers that his high school later hired him as a consultant to help them keep their very complex computer system working, during which time Stephan even designed a work from home system that benefited the school during the very challenging covid years.

Sometimes the days seemed endless; I was looking for another full-time job now that I was officially a single parent, had sold my beloved house, then gotten another job, and then bought another house solo—no small feat in real estate–challenged Los Angeles— and of course struggled with work/life balance as do so many parents, especially single mothers (drive, work, parent, sleep, repeat, this was my existence)—but the years flew by.

And suddenly Stephan was graduating from fifth grade.

How could it be? It seemed like just yesterday that he was a tiny pink baby dependent on me for virtually everything.

And now my bold, kind, smart, funny, unstoppable little boy was about to enter middle school.

STEPHAN was excited for graduation day. He even agreed to wear a polo shirt and long pants rather than his favorite funny tee-shirt and plaid shorts. As Nanny and I sat in the chairs at the assembly, the music playing softly as we waited for the students to begin their slow march to the stage, I couldn't help but tear up at the memory of what a long and winding road we had already traveled, from Brooklyn to San Francisco to Rochester and then to Russia, and then to Siberia and back to Moscow. I thought of how much I loved Stephan, of how privileged I was to have someone into whom I could pour so much emotion and care and love. Of how much I had absorbed of his dogged determination and of what a perfect fit our two personalities had been for each other on this crazy, rocky, amazing road.

But mostly, I thought of Stephan's unwavering hard work and unwillingness to quit, whatever the challenge. I hoped he would retain that tenacity as he grew, knowing that the challenges he would face would grow greater too.

I shifted in my seat and glanced over at Nanny. The music swelled and the fifth-graders began their fidgety, red-cheeked march towards the podium. Stephan looked towards me with an expression of pride and embarrassment—he had never loved being center stage—and although I think he secretly loved it, he rolled his eyes when Nanny and I clapped and cheered, "Whoo-hoo, all right Stephan!"

I could not help but marvel for the millionth time how very far Stephan had come.

The children sang an emotional song, the principal made a beautiful and inspiring speech. The moments ticked by, every parent teary-eyed.

Then it was time for each student's name to be read and for them to walk across the stage and take his or her diploma, which would hopefully be the first of many.

"Stephan Baum-Harvey," they said, and Stephan walked nervously across the platform, trying to keep from smiling, and was handed his rolled-up diploma before he joined the graduates on the other side of the stage.

The mother of one of Stephan's buddies knew his story and said to me, "You must be thrilled—here he is graduating fifth grade—imagine if he'd stayed in Russia! You saved his life." And I instinctively said the only thing that rang true for me, a sentiment that still remains seared in my heart: "Actually, he saved mine."

Never a Dull Moment...

FOLLOWING THE AFTERGLOW of Stephan's elementary school graduation, he spent the summer on the Open Charter campus at Math Camp. Among other cool adventures, the students decided what business to start (smoothies), had to figure out ingredients, cost, whether they could make a profit, etc.

I had applied to and amazingly gotten randomly picked for Stephan to attend a highly acclaimed charter school in Santa Monica we will call Old East, one that people vied and lied and cajoled to try to attend. Of course, I was thrilled and he would go, damn the crazy logistics!

I was working at a corporate music job that was very demanding and entailed a very long daily commute but I insisted on driving Stephan to the bus stop in the morning (not that I had a much choice as a single parent). The school was in a neighborhood where the residents did not welcome it, so driving up to the school at drop-off or pick-up was *verboten*—you had to be in a designated, approved carpool (and only so many vehicles were allowed to pass through) or pay $400 a year for your child to ride the bus the last mile from a designated parking lot to school, which most of us did. Pick-up was in the same designated parking lot, not at the school campus.

Old East was headed by a principal I shall call Dr. W., a mature blonde with what sounded like a Scottish accent who marched around in her elegant dresses and high heels remarking on how many students had applied to the school each year, how they were doing so well in their fundraising for the "Million Dollar Wall" (parents could make huge donations to have their names etched onto a wall in the large gathering room, though there was neither a yard nor a cafeteria nor any outdoor play area other than a skinny, filthy parking lot behind the school), and how lucky we all were to be attending.

Sixth and seventh grades were fine, with Stephan being his usual driven self, and he made some great new friends, got mostly As and Bs, and felt okay about the school. It was a constant scramble for me, with help from my mom and sister—I would drive Stephan to the school bus at 7:30 A.M., then race back home to walk the dogs before blasting out for the long commute to work. My mom or sister would meet the bus back in the designated parking lot after school and drive Stephan the five or so miles home from there, then stay with him until I got home at around 7:00 or 7:30 P.M.

The summer before eighth grade, Stephan was again attending Math Camp and looking forward to hopefully making money as a junior counselor, but after the kids did water play during that very hot first day, he came home with an earache—something he had rarely had, even as a baby—which turned into an ear infection, which turned into an acute sinus infection. All of this was made clear to me during the course of six or so weeks full of pain, doctor visits, tests, pharmacies, etc.

I quickly learned that pediatricians, like most doctors, are usually doing their best but are really just making well-educated guesses. Especially when a child has an issue that you can't see with the naked eye, there seems to be an underpinning of mistrust, i.e., *do you think it might be psychosomatic?*

Stephan had a real live sinus infection for which they prescribed strong antibiotics. It took weeks for the drugs to work, and Stephan's infection was so acute that even bright daylight seemed to make him wince.

After the first day of Math Camp, he missed virtually the entire summer, which he reluctantly spent in bed feeling lousy, going to doctor appointments, and taking handfuls of pills.

When Stephan entered eighth grade in the fall, he was still not feeling well. His sinus infection had never seemed to clear up 100 percent despite months of antibiotics. He often complained of feeling nauseous, and it irked me endlessly that some of the doctors he'd been seeing didn't seem to believe his symptoms.

After drawing literally ten vials of blood at each appointment for nearly a month, an immunologist suggested Stephan had low immunity and might need to have a type of stent inserted to boost his immune strength. I didn't like her, she was judgmental and skeptical and had a cold demeanor, but she seemed medically bright and curious. I took her suggestions with a grain of salt and got second and third opinions, no two of which agreed.

Stephan was attending school when he felt up to it, which was intermittently, and was missing a lot of days. When I went to the school to discuss how best to handle his absences, they suggested we do a 504 plan. I had never heard of one but was told that it allowed students, especially those with chronic medical conditions, to work from home whenever they needed and attend when they could. Great, I said, that sounds perfect! They told me they had the same arrangement with a few other students with medical issues and I signed on the dotted line, much relieved. They stressed that the 504 plan was legally binding, and that Stephan would have to adhere to the rules and do all of the assignments. I was not at all worried about that part—Stephan had always been very eager to please and a super-diligent student, and in terms of doing what an authority figure requested of him, he would rather lose a limb than defy a request, as though to do so were a personal failing, a character flaw, a total embarrassment.

The medical mysteries continued, with an ear infection becoming a bacterial infection in Stephan's chest that was treated with more antibiotics. The chest infection never fully cleared up and some months later, Stephan began complaining consistently of stomach pain. Stephan did months of neti pots, sinus washes, and saltwater irrigations. When we walked into our local CVS pharmacy, they knew us by name since we had been there a few days a week for nearly a year.

At around this point some of the doctors began implying that it could be psychological, which I at first considered; a fan of therapy myself, I found a pediatric therapist and cajoled Stephan into going.

"Mom, *no*, I don't need to go, I'm fine, it's just my stomach. There's nothing wrong with my head!"

"I know," I told him "But sometimes we all need an objective person to talk to, someone who might have some tools you're not aware of to make this challenging situation a bit more manageable."

Stephan was not buying my sales pitch but I was adamant, and so off we trundled.

After I had spent a few minutes in the room with Stephan and the therapist—I wanted to look into the doctor's eyes and make sure he didn't seem like a nut or in any way predatory—I left the room so Stephan could have a private session.

When they were done the doctor called me in while Stephan waited outside. "He seems fine," the doctor said. "I don't hear any underlying issues other than him being an adolescent who is sick of feeling sick. Bottom line is he just wants to be able to do normal kid stuff—play with his friends, go to school all that."

I asked if he thought that Stephan would benefit from more sessions with him and he said, "No, not unless he wants to." Obviously, Stephan did *not* want to, and so we called that psychological foray done, my mind calmed since I then felt more confident that we were leaving no stone unturned in working to solve Stephan's medical mystery.

Some of the medical doctors we saw were still insinuating that there was a psychological component to Stephan's malady, something I found increasingly infuriating. Stephan had begun needing to go to the bathroom dozens of times a day, something that was all too real and was definitely *not* imagined. He had always been a bit stoic, not one to be vocally effusive, and he never exaggerated—if Stephan said something hurt or bothered him, I knew it meant that it was real and potentially serious.

Through it all, Stephan diligently kept up his schoolwork, doing every single assignment for every subject and turning them all in via email every Friday. Despite numerous requests, I rarely heard back from individual teachers and could never reach anyone at the school on the phone, including the principal Dr. W. (from whom I continued to get plenty of fundraising and Million Dollar Wall emails).

Every single day during Stephan's very long illness felt like a year; I would leave in the morning worried about his health, call him ten times a day to check on him, terrified that something drastic would happen, that he would suddenly get much sicker, and that I would be stuck in some faraway corporate office unable to get back home to him quickly. Like so many single parents—especially mothers, in my experience—I took every single one of my own vacation and sick days to take Stephan to his endless doctor appointments or to comfort him when he was violently unwell, not to mention the many times I lied about having outside meetings whereas I was really headed to yet another doctor's appointment. When I was at work, I worried about my son; when I was at home or at a medical appointment, I worried I was slacking off at work (which was not true as I was doing an increasing workload with every passing month at the office, mostly due to chronic corporate understaffing and a team boss who functioned as regressively as if it were 1957).

The most frustrating part of the whole thing was that no two doctors seemed to agree on what his illness was, and so we had no idea what we were facing or how to make it better. I went to sleep and woke up every day with a churning, nauseous feeling and made more than a few promises to the powers that be—"Please just let Stephan get well and be healthy and I will do anything, never complain, etc."

Along the way, we went to every major pediatric hospital in the Los Angeles area, from UCLA to Long Beach to Children's Hospital, where the head pediatrician, a gray-haired doctor who looked straight out of central casting, examined Stephan and then insisted, right in front of him, that there was absolutely nothing wrong with him, that it must be in his mind.

"He has to poo twenty times a day. That is not in his mind!" I said.

At our "home" hospital, we went from pediatrics to immunology to infectious disease to gastrointestinal and back again. Still no definite information.

There was one key element that I believe helped both me and

Stephan get through every hour, minute, day and chapter of this horrible medical ordeal: Humor.

I had long said to Stephan, starting when he was around four years old during the time I was getting divorced and then shortly thereafter had to sell our beloved house, "Keep your sense of humor—it will make your life a lot easier and much more fun."

Before I sold our house, in an effort to soften the blow I had Stephan watch the movie *The Money Pit* with me, which he loved. My brother stayed over one night and together they ate three bags of cookies while watching *The Bourne Identity*, obviously very inappropriate for a toddler but still one of Stephan's fondest memories, partly because he understood how ill-suited it was for someone his age.

During the stomach illness in his eighth-grade year, I started declaring Friday night Family Movie Night and made sure we had copies of some classic, screwball comedies. I had dug up *It's a Mad, Mad, Mad, Mad World,* the *Pink Panther* films (the originals with Peter Sellars), *The Naked Gun, Airplane,* and plenty of others.

"I don't want to watch a movie, Mom, I just want to play computer games with my friends or go to bed," Stephan would say.

"Come on, just watch the first five minutes, then if you don't like it we'll turn it off." We would cozy up on the couch with a bowl of snacks and I'd hit "play."

I remember the first time we watched *Airplane,* starring Leslie Nielsen. At first Stephan was merely smiling, enjoying how overtly screwy and silly everything was. He was trying not to crack a smile— always a stoic dude, my boy—but by the time we were twenty or so minutes into it, he was laughing out loud and had forgotten about doctors and pain and shots and nutty teachers, at least momentarily. In the ensuing years, Stephan has cultivated that same goofy sense of humor, and some days after we enjoyed a new funny movie together, after which he might admit, "Yeah, it was okay," a few minutes later I'd hear him telling his friends on the phone about it, insisting that they watch it the next time they got together.

I still get a kick out of seeing Stephan understand the joke when someone says, "And don't call me Shirley."

IN our ongoing search to solve the mystery of Stephan's stomach malady, one of the doctors suggested that Stephan had the symptoms of cystic fibrosis and told us to go to the one area hospital that administered the test once a week. So I skipped another day of work and went down, telling Stephan it was a mild formality and nothing to worry about. Of course, I was terrified, and told no one in my family—what was the point? If it was negative, no reason to worry them. If it was positive, they would know soon enough.

Thankfully the test came back negative, but Stephan's acute stomach issues continued.

I went to a homeopath, an acupuncturist (they did acupressure on kids), and a very expensive family doctor who now practiced "natural medicine." After the appointment ($700 out of pocket) and another wad of cash for the doctor's own brand of supplements, none of which did any good, I called to complain about the high price and ineffective results, and the doctor said, "I'm just a family doctor—if he has stomach issues, go to a gastroenterologist." I wanted to punch him, the quack, one of the many bullshit L.A. doctors who had somehow lassoed a celebrity clientele into paying exorbitant fees for mediocre care while simultaneously shelling out thousands of dollars for an elixir that was not much different from a ten-dollar jar of multivitamins.

As much as I resented the latest charlatan doctor, I was inspired to find a pediatric gastroenterologist who then ran a whole battery of tests on Stephan, all of which came back negative. We began collecting poo samples from him to see if there were parasites or something like that, also negative. One day Stephan's belly would be normal, the next day distended as if he were a starving orphan. He wasn't sleeping much and had a spotty appetite at best. And he always, constantly, felt lousy.

Through it all, through months of humiliating tests and prodding and skeptical declarations—some doctors would talk about Stephan as if he weren't sitting right there—Stephan continued to bang out his schoolwork, never missing one single assignment.

The history teacher suggested that Stephan tackle a 500-page book on John Adams since it would cover the whole semester's worth of American history. Stephan did so. Most teachers didn't respond to my requests for updates, and when I tried to contact the school, was told they/he/she were unavailable, out of town, or both. The principal was never around, ditto the vice principal. At one point, the English teacher had changed so many times that we didn't even have a name of who it was currently supposed to be.

After months of testing and treatment, the gastro doctor said, "I can't think of anything else we haven't tested—we need to scope him." I knew he was right.

So we scheduled a dual colonoscopy/endoscopy. I downplayed it but told the basic truth to Stephan—they're going to look down your throat and up your behind to see what's going on in your stomach; you won't feel anything, they'll give you some happy juice, when you wake up a few minutes later it will be over.

Was I secretly worried? Of course! This was my little boo-boo who had already been through hell and back. He was still so little, barely thirteen years old, and he'd been going through medical challenges since he was born. I couldn't help but think back on the Brooklyn days when I would trot off down the street with my full poo specimen bag, dutifully dropping it off at the lab for the first few weeks or months, ruling out one dread disease or deficiency after another. And now here we were again…

It was only when Stephan went to sleep that I would let myself lose it, crying or quaffing a few glasses of wine. Or both. But there was always one more day, one more work event to tend to, one more doctor appointment to make, and I didn't have the luxury of falling apart. And so I didn't. Although if I had to go through the whole thing again, I don't think I could do it. It was reminiscent of the early days when Stephan had just come home and neither of us knew what dire challenges he was facing, mentally or physically. That blissful ignorance played a key role in helping us muddle through, and in hindsight here it was again (although I suppose that is how life is—you just keep going, never stopping to look back at the big picture until you have made it through whatever chapter was so challenging).

The day of Stephan's scope came and off we went early in the morning, my mother coming along for moral support. In the waiting room were a bunch of elderly men with walkers, their doting wives, and us. Little Stephan looked like a fish out of water and was nervous and cranky; he had barely slept, and clearly didn't want to be there. Who wanted a scope at all, much less one considered embarrassing enough by some grown men that they refuse to do it?

But there we were.

I went in with Stephan as they prepped him, coaxed him into changing into a hospital gown despite his protestations. Not for the first time, I couldn't help but wonder what horrific and painful memories might be embedded into that swift computer brain of his and what it evoked. Did hospital smells bring it all back, months of being plugged into machines in some anonymous ward in a small town in Russia? Of having nothing but fear and pain to drive him?

I stood by his side as the nice nurses came in and started an I.V., which set him off again as soon as the curtain closed around his gurney. He was infuriated, exhausted from months of pain and poo, and likely terrified.

"Mom, I *do not* want to do this! Why are you making me do this? I do not want to wear this gown! I hate this!"

I assured him that they were taking great care of him, that I would be right there, that he would be done quickly, and that then hopefully we would know how to help him feel better. Permanently.

When they came to wheel him away, I smiled, kissed him and waved and watched the swinging door close behind him as they disappeared into the operating theater.

I walked back out to the waiting room where Nanny sat reading, and it was then that I lost it and the tears started. He had been through so much! We had been through so much!

The receptionist called for me to come and bring my credit card, which I did.

And then I waited. What if they found something terrible, like cancer? What if there was a growth? By this point, Stephan had had CAT scans, x-rays, ultrasounds, and whatever else they could come up with, so I wasn't expecting a foreign object to be discovered, but one never knew and for a full year nothing had helped him get better.

The time passed slowly. I paced the waiting room, my mom coaxing me to relax but to no avail.

"Alexandra, Alexia Baum?" The nurse said through the open door. I leapt up and ran into the recovery area. There the gastroenterologist said that in Stephan he had discovered the worst *H. pylori* infection he had ever seen in his life, in a grownup or a child. "I can't believe he's able to even walk around like this," the doctor said.

He showed me pictures that the scopes had taken, all the way from Stephan's esophagus to colon, and where it should have been smooth and pink, it was lumpy and inflamed. "See this?" the doctor said pointing at what looked like a lumpy moonscape—"this should all be smooth...poor kid..."

"Oh my God," I said.

Stephan was by that point wide awake, smiling, sipping juice, and sitting up. "That wasn't so bad," he said. "I don't remember anything."

In a way it was a relief—finally, after so much searching, we knew that what Stephan was suffering from was (a) real, and (b) treatable.

H. Pylori

HELICOBACTER PYLORI (*H. pylori*) is a very common type of bacterium, and about two-thirds of the world's population have it in their bodies. It is caused by germs that enter your body and live in your digestive tract. After time, they can cause sores or ulcers in the lining of your stomach or the upper part of your small intestine. For most people, the bacteria don't cause ulcers or any other symptoms; if you do have problems, there are medicines that can kill the germs and help heal sores. For some people, an infection can lead to stomach cancer.

But poor little Stephan, he had gotten a giant dose! No doubt, the year of strong antibiotics that had been used to cure his ear infection, then his sinus infection, and then the bacterial infection in his chest, had weakened his stomach to the point that the germs a kid would usually fight off were able to infect him and wreak havoc.

There was and may still yet be one single prescribed protocol to cure *H. pylori*, which could not go untreated lest you risk having it develop into something worse, like stomach cancer. And that cure was—you guessed it—more antibiotics!

Stephan was to take a cocktail of pills, about fifteen a day, for two weeks.

"Fifteen pills!" I exclaimed when Stephan was out of earshot. "He's just a kid—don't these come in liquid form?" No was the short answer, and we simply couldn't screw around with this infection—it had

clearly been in there for quite a while and done more than enough damage.

And so back to CVS we went, waiting while they filled bag after bag with pill bottles, then spent fifteen minutes explaining what had to be taken in what order, etc.

As soon as we got in the car to go home, Stephan said, "No way! I am *not* doing that! I don't care, I've had enough!"

I couldn't blame him and in fact felt the same way, but we had no choice. There were some homeopathic and organic things to try—manuka honey, teas, and the like—but Stephan's case was so extreme that I didn't want to waste time when he was still in so much pain. We were going full force with treatment.

On day one, I said, "The sooner we start, the sooner it's over and behind you." To his credit, Stephan gulped down one horse-size pill after another, almost retching but not quite, until the whole morning's dose had been taken, a huge handful of pills.

Great job! I hugged Stephan before he stomped down the hallway and flopped onto his bed.

This went on three times a day for two weeks. Pill after handful of pills, constant nausea, constant trips to the bathroom, no discernible positive change in how Stephan felt. And all the while he kept plugging away at schoolwork, turning in every assignment every week with little to no feedback from his teachers.

At the end of the designated treatment, two weeks of three doses of pills a day, we collected another stool sample and dropped it off at the lab (it was the best way to test for the presence of *H. pylori*). I drove away happily, sure that the worst would now be behind Stephan and we could concentrate on healing.

But a few days later when the doctor called, he said, "I'm so sorry, but the test came back positive; Stephan still has the infection. You need to repeat the course of antibiotics."

"Oh no!" I wailed. "Are you sure? Any chance of a mix-up? Is there any other way to get rid of this? I really hate to put Stephan through this again. The pills are impossible to swallow, they make him gag, make him nauseous, it's horrible." I had talked to one forty-something-year-old man who had stopped taking the pills, they made him so miserable.

But there was no other way and so we went back to the pharmacy and I broke the news to Stephan. Again he wailed and railed against it and again I didn't blame him. But again we launched into it on day one, and every single day Stephan ingested about fifteen pills, felt seasick, was irritated and cranky, and made it through the two-week period.

Again, we took a specimen bag to the lab, and again I drove away feeling optimistic that we would get good news a week later.

But it was not to be. Again, the doctor called and said the test was positive. "No," I said, "I do not want to put Stephan through this again! I can't ask him to do it, it's torture! Can you consult with another doctor? Is there an alternate protocol?" I had done nightly online research and had lots of ideas, but the bottom line seemed to be that the antibiotic treatment was the key, and although you couldn't eliminate any of the few prescribed medicines in the cocktail, you could slightly tweak the dose of each one. The doctor assured me he had consulted with lots of experts—and I had consulted our regular pediatrician, the immunologist, even a few doctors I didn't know—and tweaked the dosage slightly.

"We have to eliminate the infection," the doctor said, "we can't let it linger there because it could cause stomach cancer. It's not likely," he added, "but we have to get rid of the infection. That's the bottom line."

When I went back to CVS for a third round of the many bags of antibiotics, they said, "We're so sorry. Good luck!"

I couldn't believe he actually raised the pills to his lips and swallowed them down again, but my game, tough, stubborn little Stephan did. Every day, three times a day. I had read where many grownups refused to take the course of drugs, so nasty were they. But somehow each dose went down and in a drug-induced time warp, the two weeks were up.

Back to the lab with my brown bag of goodies.

A week later, another call from the doctor. *Still positive.*

"Oh no!" I wailed. "I can't, I won't put Stephan through this again!"

"I am not sure how else to help you," the doctor said. "You probably want to try another physician; good luck."

I hung up and sent an email to good old Dr. Aronson, the New York City pediatrician who had advised us during Stephan's adoption from Russia. Granted she hadn't laid eyes on Stephan in over a decade, but I inherently trusted her and she was an expert on all kinds of strange international bugs and diseases.

I simultaneously contacted an infectious disease specialist at UCLA, and when Dr. Aronson scoffed at Stephan having been treated unsuccessfully three times, she suggested a specific tweak to the dosage, which I relayed to the infectious disease doctor.

A week later, Stephan began yet another round of antibiotics to cure his still-raging *H. pylori* infection. Same pills, slightly different dosage.

I didn't even have any platitudes to offer Stephan. This course of treatment utterly sucked, there were no two ways about it. But we had no better options so on we went.

After two weeks of swallowing impossible, horse-sized pills three times a day, I took Stephan's poo back to the lab. I was limp, I didn't feel hopeful or positive, it was reminiscent of the hopelessness I had felt fifteen years earlier when I had been trying so desperately to become a mother. But dutifully, off I went.

I was at work when the doctor called me. "The test was negative."

"Oh my God!" I screamed so loudly that some of my co-workers came running towards my office. "Are you sure?" I asked.

She assured me that the infection had been killed off, and after I hung up and could stop sobbing long enough to catch my breath, I started thinking about ways we could try to heal Stephan's battle-weary gut and exhausted body.

A for Awesome, D for Determined

MEANWHILE, THE ISSUES with school and their lack of communication continued to mount, and one particularly sadistic teacher, whom I will call Mr. H., had been appointed head of the eighth-grade class. He was the one who had suggested that Stephan read the 500-page John Adams book, and then denied having received the very long essay Stephan wrote about it. Stephan redid the essay and I watched as he hit "send." Mr. H. again denied receiving it. And on it went. He was a teacher who should not have been a teacher and seemed to delight in humiliating students.

To make a very long and arduous story short, at the end of the school year the school denied that Stephan had done all the assignments necessary ("But look, here's copies of every single piece of work he sent in," I said), and they denied granting him credit to enter ninth grade.

I was incensed. After numerous phone calls, the principal and Mr. H. finally agreed to meet with me; during the meeting Mr. H. accused Stephan of being a liar and a plagiarist, neither of which has ever been remotely true. The principal, Dr. W., suggested that Stephan attend a continuation school for kids who couldn't cut it in regular school. When I protested and reminded them that it was *their* idea to do a 504 plan, Dr. W. looked me in the eyes and said, *"We are a site-based school."*

My mom, who had accompanied me and who is herself a retired

teacher, had to hold me back as I had an overwhelming urge to rip Mr. H.'s smirk off his face.

After the meeting, when I had cooled down a bit, I called a friend who runs a preschool and she suggested a firm of attorneys that handle children's rights within the education system, something it is appalling to think we even need.

I gave the attorneys all the information of what had transpired and they said they would definitely take our case and would fight not for monetary damages but for Stephan to be granted a year's worth of education in the form of tutoring, something they were by law obligated to have offered us during his long illness (something about which I had no idea, another area in which our education is seriously lacking).

Looking back, I can't help but wince a bit when I think of all the information I lacked; I did not know that I was entitled to have a teacher come to our house during Stephan's illness (and the school never offered). I should have been more skeptical about the skills of our attorneys, who, after a year's worth of testing and paperwork and maneuvering, won our case (we were granted a certain number of tutoring hours to be paid by the school/district), but lost the war (they blew it and by the time the paperwork was signed, there was only a month left to fulfill all the hours, which was a virtual impossibility).

Mind you, a tutor had been coming to our house twice a week for much of the year to bolster Stephan's schooling, and after the debacle of Old East, I asked what he thought about having Stephan move on to ninth grade, high school, versus the idea of repeating the eighth grade via home schooling. The tutor suggested the latter.

"It really isn't fair to expect Stephan to know everything you learn in eighth grade since he had virtually no instruction," he offered, "especially since he will be expected to have all this information in high school." I could not disagree. I planned on Stephan repeating eighth grade so that he could later enter high school fully up to speed and with every chance of succeeding. It was an idea, repeating eighth grade, that I knew he would hate.

During that summer, what should have been in between eighth and ninth grades, Stephan was having increasingly serious stomach issues, which turned out to be acute infection-driven irritable bowel syndrome, or IBS, possibly as a result of having been on all the antibiotics needed to cure the *H. pylori. Great,* I thought, *what more can this poor kid take!*

And so over the next few months we embarked on a new round of doctor visits, from a teen clinic at UCLA, to an IBS clinic, to Chinese herb doctors, you name it (gotta love those out-of-pocket medical expenses). Eventually we found a cocktail composed of a low-dose IBS drug combined with a medical-strength probiotic that seemed to help, and along with his being gluten- and lactose-free, Stephan's very painful and inconvenient stomach issues slowly, slowly began to seem manageable.

Through all of this, Stephan was home schooling via an official California home school company and their website. He would have some class time with teachers live online and then complete homework and other assignments on his own. I was apprehensive about the whole thing, especially as I was continuing to work and commute long hours, but with regular support from my mom and sister, Stephan proved once again that he had a rock-solid work ethic and was an academic standout; he was always prepared, on time, respectful, and loved to work ahead of the study plan. He even made the honor roll and was given awards for citizenship and leadership, the awards a bit of salve on his unfairly bruised psyche following the mistreatment he had received from Old East. (It did help that we sometimes joked about leaving a doggie bag of poo on the front steps of their oh-so-precious charter school, something we would never really do in real life, but it made us both giggle during stressful times to imagine running up and hurling it towards their door.)

Ultimately Stephan made it very successfully through his year of official home schooling, and when I heard about a well-loved local charter school that was expanding on their elementary and middle schools to open a brand-new high school, I leapt at the chance to enroll Stephan. I turned in all the paperwork and made friends with the woman in the school office, gently pestering her until we found out that Stephan would indeed be admitted and would be attending ninth grade at the school that fall.

We were both nervous, Stephan and I—what if he had a bad stomach day, what if he had to use the restroom super-suddenly?—but I assured Stephan that the school knew his challenges and were happy to accommodate them.

That was now more than four years ago, and I am thrilled to say that since then, Stephan has excelled academically—including making the national honor roll, frequently taking extracurricular college-level classes, taking advanced placement classes, and independently pursuing and obtaining his commercial drone pilot's license—kept a great circle of friends as well as a long-term girlfriend, started and nurtured a few online video game design and coding businesses, and all in all become a feisty, smart, strong teenager. All of which goes to show that the little signs I put up in his room, NEVER NEVER NEVER GIVE UP and HAPPINESS IS A CHOICE, were right all along. And there have been plenty of times that I needed to go in and reread those signs myself just to keep marching.

Mostly what has kept me going is Stephan—his tenacity, his drive, his smarts. Although of course there were plenty of the normal, way less fun aspects of parenting too. The day Stephan turned sixteen, it was like someone pushed a switch and he suddenly, totally transformed into Surly Teen, replete with, "How could you possibly be so utterly lame, Mom?" eyerolls, requests to get out of his room and shut the door on my way out, and promises that he would clean his clothes off his invisible floor soon, aka never. In other words, he was a regular teenager.

Some days, after an especially challenging interaction, I would remind myself that this was what I had wished for during all those years of not only my baby quest but also during his illnesses, during the countless days, weeks, months of waiting in the lobbies of doctors' offices, of forcing the poor kid to ingest some new pill or liquid or potion. Normalcy. And that even though there were moments when I wanted to reach out and wrap my hands around his smirking little teenaged throat—picture an exaggerated comic book or the Three Stooges—the attitude was Stephan's way of starting to break away from the mothership, of declaring his selfhood, his presence on the planet (albeit unconsciously). It was nature's way of softening the blow for later when he does fly the nest and leave for college, not to mention that it gave me as a mother the mental space to start imagining him leaving and not feeling too bad about it, and on some especially challenging days, to even relish the thought.

But on those special days when I would get the triple-header of mega-smirk, eyeroll, and demand that I leave his room, I reminded myself of everything he and I had been through, sometimes giving him an unwelcome giant hug and kiss as I exited, something that irked him but that I told myself he secretly loved. Or I at least hoped that I was storing up a great stockpile of love in him, knowing that he would need the reserves as he ventured out into the big, bad world.

After all, that is what this whole journey has been about, right? Love. My desire to love someone, something, Stephan's need as a baby the same as every baby on the planet, to have someone dedicated to providing that love, that protection, that blind devotion, along with all the necessities that come along with it like food, shelter, medical care, and the like.

I recognize how lucky we have been even in our most challenging times. I have been able to provide Stephan with great housing, good public schools, and top-notch medical care—too many families don't have all those options, and that is a societal shame and something that desperately needs fixing. I must also add that, despite our marriage ending years ago amidst some seriously overwhelming issues, as well as long periods of David being absent from Stephan's daily world, David has remained a positive presence in Stephan's life—weekend lunches, movies, other fun outings—and for that I am grateful.

Call it a maternal instinct. Call it the better aspects of human nature, this irresistible drive we often bear to nurture another being in such a desperately devoted way. Parenting, especially when children are infants and babies, necessitates such acts of devotion, and that deep, selfless, absolute love tends to brand our hearts in the best possible way. It is my hope that once we have borne that feeling, that totality of commitment, that love and joy and frustration and sense of permanence, knowing that no matter what, no matter the lows or highs, we are there for the long haul, unshakably attached to this other being, that we are capable of restocking that shelf once our babies are grown up. That we as humans can, consciously or not, later access that place of total love and vulnerability and strength. Which is a place from which we can connect and love deeply, not just our children, but our families, friends, co-workers, selves, and others.

And that is what I remember, more than the hours and days and years of early intervention, more than the chronic illnesses and battles with schools unworthy of Stephan's deep drive and intelligence, certainly more than the teenage eyerolls; I remember the sweetness and depth of our connection. I remember Stephan's terrified but acutely aware expression when I first laid eyes on him in the room of the orphanage in Ramenskoye, Russia, of my instinctively muttering, "He's alive." I remember days of pushing Stephan's stroller down the tree-lined streets of Brooklyn, smiling as I chatted away, thrilled when Stephan *oohe*d and *aahe*d at every truck or fire engine that rolled past. I remember his unwavering determination as he defied the dire predictions of his early years, the glee of his discovery of Elmo, the way he would always sit in the front row of his classroom in elementary school and be the first to volunteer to help a teacher or a friend.

Stephan thrived in high school, and even oversaw his school's vast and endless tech needs, represented his school at the citywide political district meetings, and was a proud member of the National Honor Society, among other things. I think of his Birth Mother every August 9 and imagine that she must be wondering if he is alive and whatever became of him. I have told Stephan all I know about his background, including that he may have two full siblings in Russia—one can never be certain if the documents we were given are accurate—and that I would be happy to go with him to look them all up one day. As of now, he says he is not interested.

With his drive and smarts, Stephan continues to defy both those who wished him well but thought he might never be fully mentally or physically cognizant, as well as those who insisted there was something amiss with him when I was sure they were mistaken and that they simply hadn't taken the time to really *see* him. And I will be forever grateful for everyone who supported and cajoled and taught and challenged him along the way, those teachers, grandparents, friends, and family. It really does take a village!

I remember the absolute love I felt and still feel for Stephan, a love that has enriched and helped define my life and made me eternally grateful to have had the privilege of finding Stephan, of us finding each other, and having served as the launchpad into the rest of his life.

Epilogue

I PULL TO A FULL STOP as the light flashes from orange to red. Once my car rocks slightly backwards into a full stop, I glance down at my pinging phone.

"What the...?"

It looks like a college acceptance letter. Stephan, eighteen years old, having spent his senior year of high school working from home amidst the Covid-19 lockdown, is in the midst of the insane American ritual of college acceptance season. Or un-acceptance, aka rejection season. A tough and seemingly random season to be sure.

I squint at the phone, glance up to check the stoplight is still red. What does that tiny insignia say on the upper left side of the letter? University of California something or other—Stephan has decided that he wants to stay in our home state of California for college and applied to many UC schools—I raise the phone closer to my face and mumble as I read.

"University of California Berkeley." What? Holy crap!

The car behind me tap taps their horn and I throw my phone down and tend to driving across the busy intersection until I can pull onto a quieter side street. I grab my phone and auto-dial Stephan, who picks up on the first ring.

"Did you just get into freakin' *Berkeley*?" I half shout.

"Yes, Mom." Effusive communication is not the hallmark of many teenage males and the same goes for Stephan.

"Oh—my—*God!*" The tears start to roll down my face.

"Mom, please," Stephan mutters but I can hear in his voice that he is smiling and proud.

"Oh, honey, I can't believe it, you've worked so hard and been through so much…"

"Okay, Mom, I'm at work, I'll see you later. Love you." The phone hangs up.

Wow, wow, U.C. Berkeley! I am even more thrilled for Stephan when I read the acceptance letter, which is one of the most poignant and heartfelt letters I have ever seen, even more surprising to see coming from a major university (and lucky timing for us, U.C. Berkeley was then rated the year's number one university).

As I drive home, I cannot help but reflect back on some of the many trials and tribulations of Stephan's young life, of our lives together, and indeed of the many years it took for us to become a family. As I pull into our driveway, the last eighteen years start to run through my mind like an old newsreel. This is one of those big moments, a milestone, a happy crossroad in Stephan's young life and in our life as a family, and one that makes my looking backwards inevitable.

I thought back over the two decades since I launched into my years-long quest for family, during which I endured an ectopic pregnancy, numerous failed IVF cycles, and ten—yes ten—fruitless domestic adoption scenarios. Not to mention our misadventure to Siberia in the dead of winter. By the time I finally met Stephan literally on the other side of the planet in an orphanage fifty-five miles and 100 years outside of Moscow, it had seemed like a surreal dream.

I had been aware of Stephan's rough start in life, the fact that he had been a hidden pregnancy, that he was born two months premature and spent the first six months of his life in the neonatal intensive care unit with pneumonia so severe that each day he was still alive was a surprise. But I had been too naïve to be scared off, and too exhausted from the years-long search not to mention too in love with the idea of motherhood, with the bliss of finally perhaps having found a being I could love completely and who needed me. And from the very first moment I laid eyes on him, it was clear that Stephan was a fighter.

Stephan has never lost that defiant spirit, a trait we share and which he quickly proved he has in spades. Not only did he give Pavarotti a run for his money by squalling at the top of his tiny nine-month-old lungs during the entire flight from Moscow home to New York but he stared down innumerable childhood illnesses and defied every dire prediction about how he would be hard pressed to ever develop normally, to walk, talk, or function on a level with his peers. Really? He needs early intervention twice a day, five days a week in every area, speech, special ed, physical, and occupational therapies? Um, okay…

As I had become an unwitting expert in the world of early intervention, I had secretly thought, *but you are wrong, all you experts, look at this beautiful boy! His innate intelligence, his sheer grit! He is going to be better than fine…*

And now here we are, looking ahead towards college, and I can't help but laugh at the absurdly long, sometimes ridiculous, often heartbreaking but ultimately incredible journey we have shared, and to marvel once again at Stephan's innate drive and how he has already had to work harder in his young life than many of us do in a lifetime.

Anyone in their right mind could ask of me in this story, *were you insane, way back when you were trying to get pregnant, then trying to adopt? Why on earth would you put yourself through all of that, year after year?* No, I don't think I was insane, I was just single-mindedly determined to become a mother. You could not throw anything at me; no roadblock, no matter how absurd, would deter me from my quest, just as apparently nothing could shake the determination out of Stephan from the moment he was born, despite the overwhelming odds stacked against him.

Looking back on it all, as well as living it every day, the pride and love I have for Stephan, the joy motherhood still brings me, the stubborn determination that colors both our personalities, the crazy, circuitous route it took for us to connect, to find each other—I am eternally proud and grateful that neither Stephan nor I ever gave up in our journey to find each other and become a family.

A Final Note on Russian Adoption

IN DECEMBER 2012, Vladimir Putin made it impossible for Americans to adopt children from Russia. (Russian Federal law number 272-FZ remains in place banning the adoption of Russian children by U.S. citizens.) It was in retaliation against the U.S., which had justly reacted to the torture and murder of a Russian whistleblower by enacting the Magnitsky Act, which banned the implicated Russian officials from traveling to the U.S., owning property, or having bank accounts. And in the intervening years, the relationship between our two countries has grown even more strained. Even when I was there in 2003, it was uncomfortably clear that, as an American, I was perceived as rich and privileged (though by comparison I suppose it was true) and was mostly unwelcome to the point of hostility from many native Russians.

But as one of the Russian adoption agency representatives in Moscow had said, "When Russians get mad at Americans adopting Russian babies, I say to them, 'Then adopt them yourself!'"

Abortion was still mostly taboo in 2003 and religion was still a strong component of society. And women's rights, including the ability to openly discuss and treat any type of infertility, were pretty much nonexistent. Not to mention the country's chronic levels of alcoholism and unemployment. Suffice to say, there were plenty of issues that had led to the hundreds of thousands of babies and children languishing in under-supported orphanages across the vast country. And dropping off one's baby or child at an orphanage to get three meals a day, with the intent of picking them up and bringing them home when one's economic situation improved, seemed to still be an acceptable part of society (as my Russian immigrant grandmother had done with my mother and her brother in Chicago during the Depression). Whether this sad cocktail of dire conditions still persists in Russia nearly twenty years since I was there, I do not know for certain, but given the state of their government, I would be surprised if things had evolved much.

From 1982 to 2012, roughly 60,000 Russian orphans had been adopted by Americans, and although there were a handful of cases of abuse, each one a tragedy, the majority of these adoptees found forever homes in American families. The truth is, there is no guarantee that a family will be a happy one, whether you birth a child or adopt them. But I can attest first hand that one does not undertake or complete an international adoption easily or quickly or cheaply. You have got to want it extremely badly, and the vetting process is enormously in-depth, to put it mildly.

I believe we need to take the *business* out of adoption, and give qualified and capable parents, even those who are not wealthy, the ability to adopt and parent children who are languishing without homes. Further, we need to support women in Russia and China and the U.S. and worldwide to both have the ability to take care of their own bodies, be it through education and healthcare and access to birth control, as well as the ability to feed and clothe and have help caretaking their children when they do want to raise them.

In Russia, when I asked our young agency rep what would happen to the many children who did not find homes outside the orphanages, she said, "Usually, they stay in the home until they are about sixteen years old, and then they are sent out to live on their own." I asked if they had been to school and received an education, if they had been taught a trade or had any work skills at all. *"Nyet,"* she said sadly. Too many of these kids end up in prostitution, in the child sex slave market, or as homeless alcoholics, a fate individually tragic but also socially irresponsible, expensive, and unsustainable.

Sadly, the world has in some ways become even more contentious since Stephan came home from Russia, and I have no high hopes that the hundreds of thousands of Russian orphans scattered across that vast continent are faring any better these days.

But politicians eventually get replaced and regimes change, and my hope is that the emphasis will shift from macho state pride and tit-for-tat payback to actually prioritizing the needs and lives of these and other desperately needy children. And that any person, regardless of wealth or geography or whom they love, as long as they are kind and emotionally capable, will be able to make a family with a Russian—or any other child—who so desperately needs one.

www.ingramcontent.com/pod-product-compliance
Lightning Source LLC
Chambersburg PA
CBHW020322180726
47991CB00018B/224